THE BOUNDS OF REASON

In *The Bounds of Reason: Habermas, Lyotard and Melanie Klein on Rationality* Emilia Steuerman explores the limits and meaning of rationality as a tool for understanding truth, justice and freedom. She presents the current controversy between modernism and postmodernism in a rigorous yet accessible analysis of the debate between Jurgen Habermas and Jean-François Lyotard.

Steuerman clearly highlights the problems encountered both by a defence of reason and the lack of meaning which haunts a world without reason. Her goal is to ascertain whether reason can be used as a weapon of domination or as a means of emancipation, and she investigates the limits of both the rationalist and irrationalist projects by introducing the work of the psychoanalyst Melanie Klein. Klein's theory of object-relations paves the way for an understanding of the ethical and emotional bounds which hold individuals in contact with the outside world and secure our capacity for rational thought. Steuerman demonstrates how Melanie Klein's theory sheds new light onto Habermas's modernist concepts of intersubjectivity and communities of shared language users whilst also taking into account the irrational and primitive worlds of love and hatred which colour our perceptions of ourselves and others.

Emilia Steuerman has lectured in philosophy and the social sciences at Brunel University and at the Catholic University of Rio de Janiero (PUC-RJ)

PROBLEMS OF MODERN EUROPEAN THOUGHT
Series Editors
Alan Montefiore
Jonathan Rée
Jean-Jacques Lecercle

THE BOUNDS OF REASON

Habermas, Lyotard and Melanie Klein
on rationality

Emilia Steuerman

London and New York

First published 2000
by Routledge
11 New Fetter Lane, London EC4P 4EE

Simultaneously published in the USA and Canada
by Routledge
29 West 35th Street, New York, NY 10001

Routledge is an imprint of the Taylor & Francis Group

© 2000 Emilia Steuerman

Typeset in Times New Roman by Bookcraft Ltd, Stroud
Printed and bound in Great Britain by MPG Books, Bodmin

British Library Cataloguing in Publication Data
A catalogue record for this book is available from the British Library

Library of Congress Cataloging in Publication Data
CIP data have been applied for

ISBN 0-415-22267-2 (hbk)
ISBN 0-415-22268-0 (pbk)

Transcendental illusion, on the other hand, does not cease even when we have already uncovered it and have, through transcendental critique, had distinct insight into its nullity. (An example is the illusion in the proposition that the world must have a beginning in terms of time.) The cause of this is that in our reason (regarded subjectively as a human cognitive power) there lie basic rules and maxims of its use that have entirely the look of objective principles; and through this it comes about that the subjective necessity of a certain connection of our concepts for the benefit of understanding is regarded as an objective necessity of the determination of things in themselves. This is an *illusion* that we cannot at all avoid any more than we can avoid the illusion that the sea seems to us higher in the centre than at the shore because we see the centre through higher light rays than the shore; or – better yet – any more than even the astronomer can prevent the moon from seeming larger to him as it rises, although he is not deceived by this illusion.

Kant, *Critique of Pure Reason*

CONTENTS

EDITORS' FOREWORD

During most of the twentieth century, philosophers in the English-speaking world have had only partial and fleeting glimpses of the work of their counterparts in continental Europe. In the main, English-language philosophy has been dominated by the exacting ideals of conceptual analysis and even of formal logic, whilst 'Continental philosophy' has ventured into extensive substantive discussions of literary, historical, psychoanalytical and political themes. With relatively few exceptions, the relations between the two traditions have been largely uncomprehending and hostile.

In recent years, however, Continental writers such as Heidegger, Adorno, Sartre, de Beauvoir, Habermas, Foucault, Althusser, Lacan and Derrida have been widely read in English translation, setting the terms of theoretical debate in such fields as literature, social theory, cultural studies, Marxism and feminism. The suspicions of the analytical philosophers have not, however, been pacified; and the import of such Continental philosophy has mostly been isolated from original philosophical work in English.

The *Problems of Modern European Thought* series is intended to help break down this isolation. The books in the series will be original philosophical essays in their own right, from authors familiar with the procedures of analytical philosophy. Each book will present a well-defined range of themes from Continental philosophy, and will presuppose little, if any, formal philosophical training of its readers.

Alan Montefiore
Jonathan Rée
Jean-Jacques Lecercle

ACKNOWLEDGEMENTS

I would like to thank Alan Montefiore for his continuous support throughout the writing of this book. His seminars at Balliol, where he brought together the British and the Continental traditions of philosophy, were inspiring. I am profoundly indebted to his generosity, his patience and his intellectual rigour.

I also wish to thank my students and colleagues at PUC/Rio Philosophy Department, especially Eduardo Jardim de Moraes, Danilo Marcondes de Souza and Wilson Pessoa de Mendonça, who saw the beginnings of this work; John Hayes, who supervised my Ph.D. and introduced me to the Anglo-Saxon world; Jean Cohen, Axel Honneth, John Keane, Albrecht Wellmer, Joel Whitebook, Nancy Wood and the participants of the Dubrovnik seminars; Ana Maria Nicolaci da Costa and Servulo Augusto Figueira, who asked me to write on Habermas and psychoanalysis; and students and colleagues at Brunel University, who provided a creative environment. I feel particularly grateful to Adam Kuper for his ability to navigate between and across the boundaries of academic disciplines. Jean-François Lyotard was kind enough to clarify certain points.

Finally, reading psychoanalytical literature and undergoing analysis have changed my thoughts about thinking. There are no words to express my gratitude to Jane Temperley, Iain Dresser and Anne Alvarez. Richard Rusbridger helped me with some important Kleinian distinctions. My husband, Martin Kinston, read endless versions, suggested books and never tired of listening and discussing. My daughters made me stop. My father would have enjoyed seeing the work done. My thanks to them all.

INTRODUCTION

When I first started teaching a Philosophy of Science course in the 1970s in Brazil, the main challenge I faced was how to undermine the seemingly unshakeable faith of the first year students in what they understood to be 'science'. The French-influenced Brazilian philosophical culture was more congenial to a critique of science along the lines of Bachelard, Koyré and Canguilhem, and to this day I remember the thrill of a lecture by Foucault who, following Nietzsche, announced to a baffled – but nevertheless enraptured – audience, that 'truth' was a human invention.[1] Once a very naïve view of science was questioned, the vistas seemed infinite. I remember using in my lectures a short story by J.L. Borges, where the attempt to draw a comprehensive map of the world had to include the map-maker drawing himself drawing the map, and therefore the reader had to consider the impossibility of a fully comprehensive correspondence between the map and the natural reality it attempted to depict. Although Borges was a master of deception, excelling at creating imaginary infinite labyrinths out of actually very confined spaces, there was indeed, at that time, an almost vertiginous awareness of the immensity of possibilities opened up by the critique of science and scientific rationality, regardless of their future consequences. The recognition of the role of the map-maker, that is, of language and culture, created a space for questioning what rationality and human subjectivity could possibly mean, and this pointed to an idea of freedom and emancipation extremely important in a country dominated at the time by a military dictatorship.

There were, of course, numerous problems created by the discovery that language and human subjectivity are at the core of our ideas of truth and freedom, including the capacity we seem to have for holding on to a naïve belief, in one form or another, in a naturally given, theory-unladen reality. The plight of the cartographer in Borges's story can mislead us into the idea that a man or a group could have access to reality in its naked form and that although he (or it) could recognize the problems involved in the actual drawing of the map, he (or it) would nevertheless be able to look at reality from a vantage point. This is, unfortunately, a misreading of the story. The cartographer is never outside the map. His problem is not just how to produce a map that would include himself in the process of drawing 'reality'; his predicament is how to survive the realization that he is himself already in the map, a drawn figure drawing himself. Indeed, an insufficiently criticized understanding of language and human subjectivity as naturally given can surreptitiously reintroduce the old forms of scientism or positivism. I do not think it was a coincidence that the Brazilian Left favoured the Althusserian reading of the writings of Bachelard, an interpretation that made popular the idea of a radical epistemological rupture between science (truth) and ideology (false veil). The avant-garde could then hold on to the illusion of knowing the truth, of holding the keys to the best possible map. The problem, as we unfortunately know, is that this illusion has sometimes to resort to force in order to maintain itself as the truth. In the first chapter, I discuss in greater depth the problems arising from an insufficient critique of scientific rationality, but it is important to mention here another set of problems generated by this critique.

In the 1980s, after obtaining my doctorate, I started teaching in England, at Brunel University. Although I was aware of the impact Popper, Kuhn and even Feyerabend had had on the English-speaking world, I was quite unprepared for the widespread scepticism of and suspicion towards science and the idea of a universal (rather than a culturally relative) truth amongst the students of the human sciences. The contempt they seemed to have for science and truth created a different pedagogical challenge from the one I had encountered before in Brazil. But, to my surprise, I found that there was a symmetrical complementarity between my English and my Brazilian students that revealed their shared assumptions. Indeed, if every text is just one story among other possible stories, as my students argued, why read the recommended authors, even if they had initiated the critique of science that led to this disenchanted relativism? This apparently radical position harboured a very conservative core. Whilst 'theories' and 'old masters' were easily disposed of, naïve beliefs abounded. These very bright human science students thought that 'experience' with youth groups or community work was meaningful in itself, untainted by theoretical distortions. I realized that the disenchantment and scepticism were directed towards our Western culture with its emphasis on scientific and technological rationalities, whilst other cultures or minority groups within our societies were perceived to be pure and true. The problem, however, is that if we go back to the idea that there is a reality (science for my Brazilian students, distant tribes or Black and women's groups for my English students) outside language, then we have no criteria – philosophically or politically – for questioning, say, National Front groups, or the fundamentalism and oppressive features of non-Western groups. Our ideas of truth, justice and freedom, culturally identified with Western scientific rationality and forms of domination, are irredeemably tainted.

This general atmosphere of distrust of theories was particularly damaging for the human and social sciences, for now, as distinct from the 1960s and 1970s, what was at stake was more than their scientificity, an already endangered criterion. What was now being questioned was the very core of what the human sciences stood for, namely the idea that human action has a meaning, and that what gives meaning to our lives is the never-ending task of seeking understanding through interpretations. In this sense, the case of psychoanalysis is exemplary for, as a discipline and in its practice, it emphasizes the role of meaning even in what we had thought was meaningless (jokes, dreams) or in what we had understood to be the domain of natural science (Freud's hysterics and what we now think of as psychosomatic illnesses). As a clear example of what a science of the human psyche could be, psychoanalysis was criticized, in the 1960s and 1970s, for its lack of 'hard' scientific credentials, that is, for its departure and distinction from the natural sciences.[2] With the general acceptance of the role of language and interpretation in the natural sciences that followed, there came a recognition of the role played by language and interpretation in every science. The attack on psychoanalysis then shifted to its allegedly questionable efficiency and validity (to be measured, however, following parameters more akin to the medical sciences), and even to Freud's honesty and integrity. Jeffrey Masson's books[3] provide a good example, because they illustrate the particular twist involved in the denial of the meaning of human action.

According to Masson, Freud was a coward who backtracked and covered up the evidence of sexual abuse he had found, in order to give scientific credibility to his new discipline and gain acceptance among his peers. That such a critique could be taken seriously is indeed surprising, given the much greater difficulties Freud had to face with his unpopular and controversial concept of the unconscious. But it is probable that Masson found an audience precisely because his argument undermined the idea of the unconscious in favour of the harsh 'reality' of what had happened, that is, the alleged sexual abuse. Freud's genius, however, was his understanding of the relevance of our unconscious ways of perceiving the world. These fantasies are not a 'made-up' world, but the real world of mental life which gives meaning and colour to reality. The horror of abuse, when indeed it happens, is even more devastating once we acknowledge the reality of mental and emotional life. This acknowledgement calls our attention to the care required for the psychic — as well as the physical — damage done. Somehow, amidst the battle between the 'objectivism' of the 1960s and 1970s and the 'relativism'[4] of the 1980s and 1990s, the fundamental relevance of the meaning of our ways of perceiving and constructing the world in language was put aside. If everything is a story, then let's deal with 'realities', so the argument goes. The problem is that in so doing one is forgetting that these realities, constructed as if they existed outside our worlds, are still very much our own constructions. Psychoanalysis can tell us a lot more about the power and pain that these constructions, now seen as foreign, 'outside' objects, can have upon our lives.

In a sense, one could say that the modernity debate that became popular in the 1980s, a debate that started in the arts and subsequently became important in philosophical terms, is a continuation of the objectivism/relativism dispute, in so far as what is being questioned is still the capacity of reason for leading us to true knowledge and just norms for better lives. Indeed, Jean-François Lyotard's argument in his book *The Postmodern Condition* is that in postmodern contemporary societies, the idea of knowledge as *Bildung,* that is, as education of the spirit with a view to its emancipation from ignorance and therefore from domination, has become meaningless. Knowledge has become the interchangeable, depersonalized 'bits' of information technology and this transformation reduces it to technically useful knowledge, which is either efficient or irrelevant. Habermas's defence of modernity, however, stresses the relevance of a proper understanding of the Enlightenment tradition. This tradition, often thought of in terms of a reduction of reason to science, is, in fact, particularly in the works of Kant, an acknowledgement of the limits of scientific rationality and a recognition of the superiority and necessity of the moral and the aesthetic as rational domains. The problem, argues Lyotard, is that the recognition that there are other dimensions of reason is seen through the eyes of a unifying and totalizing scientific rationality which transforms even that which it is not into what it is. The question still remains, however, how to think this 'other' of scientific reason when thinking, and particularly thinking through concepts, is seen as a reduction of the 'other' to the same. Nevertheless, if there is a refusal of conceptualization, we are in a similar position to my students, in idealizing the 'local', the 'small narratives', but being unable to provide a critical stance when required. And, as Habermas reminds us in his profile of Heidegger, the idealization of this 'other' as a mystical 'Being' which somehow escapes that which can be known, can help to legitimize Nazi power and domination.

There is, I believe, much to be gained by a reading of psychoanalysis within this debate. Habermas and Lyotard seemed to lose some of their interest in psychoanalysis once their critique of scientific rationality was fully-established. In what follows, I examine the reasons for this abandonment as they point to the shortcomings of their projects. Freud's idea of an enquiry into the unconscious should be the epitome of modernity, for it shows what can be achieved in terms of knowledge of the unknown. Indeed, it is our idea of what knowledge of ourselves and of others is, that must change in the process of acknowledging the unconscious; and this is an overall change which involves the emotional as well as the more abstract world of cognition. This change in itself shows the limits of an overrated rationality which postmodernity, with its emphasis on art and other forms of relating, clearly illustrates. Psychoanalysis, when successful, provides insights that help check the narcissism and omnipotence of claims to knowledge – the idea that I am the cartographer drawing the map. The recognition of our dependence and vulnerability – the way in which we ourselves belong to the map – can change our ways of looking at a world that as Habermas reminds us, overemphasizes mastery, control and achievement of efficiency to the detriment of the meaning of intersubjective forms of relationship. In such a world, meaning disappears, intelligence becomes a number in an I.Q. test, the mind becomes the organic brain and human nature is reduced to a bad copy of 'natural reality': a pastiche of a still life. Needless to say, in such a world we have no time for psychoanalysis nor indeed for any type of reflection that privileges meaning and interpretation. In other words, we have very little time – or money – for the human sciences.

Although much has been written about modernity and postmodernity, there are still some very important points to be made, especially in terms of how this debate exemplifies our understanding of the value and meaning of human rationality. In the terms proposed by Habermas and Lyotard, it is clear that in order to approach reason we have to acknowledge the major feature of twentieth century philosophy, what Richard Rorty has called the 'linguistic turn'. This recognition of ourselves as linguistic beings is the realization that we are always already within the Borgesian map, without any outside point of reference. This led to a 'paradigm shift' in contemporary thought, from a philosophy centred on an isolated subjectivity (as in Descartes) to an approach that privileges the prior intersubjectivity that makes possible our identity as isolated subjects. Habermas, in particular, has taken on board the meaning of this intersubjectivity to argue the case of modernity in the most compelling way since Kant. In his work, we see what a defence of our ideas of truth, justice and freedom could become, and we are drawn into the real possibilities of reworking the project of modernity. I have tried to read Lyotard against himself, so to speak, though a lot of what he has written supports my reading of him as a partner in a dialogue on modernity who challenges and therefore responds to Habermas's 'unfinished project'. But, in so doing, I found that it was Lyotard's ideas on art and the unconscious as the 'other' of reason which were most useful, although his understanding of the unconscious was too influenced by a reading of Freud that privileges the energetic dimension of the libidinal impulses.

The Kleinian school of psychoanalysis has moved away from such a reading; it emphasizes the objects, that is, the other persons our fantasies relate to, and therefore achieves a similar paradigm shift in psychoanalysis: from an isolated subjectivity (the ego with its own unconscious libidinal impulses – the id) to the very early (indeed for some, pre-natal) unconscious forms of relating and participating in an intersubjective world. This, as well as an understanding of the destructive, envious dimension of these fantasies, can help us understand (or at least understand our wish not to understand) what this 'other' of reason could possibly be, without reducing it to formal, abstract logic.

Psychoanalysis is also pertinent to the discussion of the second shift of contemporary philosophy, though this 'ethical turn' follows rather than departs from the first, more radical, linguistic turn. Indeed, the recognition of the intersubjectivity of reason leads to an immediate concern with this intersubjective community, without which no idea of rational truth or freedom could be maintained. The idea of the ethical domain as the highest achievement of reason is, of course, central to Kant and the Enlightenment tradition. The problem is how to uphold this tradition and abandon the idea of an isolated subject in a community in favour of a community of diverse beings which creates self-contained individuals. Here again I believe Kleinian psychoanalysis can contribute to the ethical discussion. It shows how even in our most 'inner' core – our 'own' private minds — indeed, even as pre-verbal infants, we are already part of an emotional and cognitive web of interrelations. This recognition exposes our dependence and reliance on others in order to be and to become autonomous selves. Therefore the more traditional ethical idea of freedom as autonomy has to be articulated with the concern for others, that is, through the idea of solidarity.

Kleinian thought helps us to think of another person as an 'other' than ourselves by drawing our attention to the unconscious, narcissistic wishes to reduce the variety of experience to what we already know. The denial of the different needs, fantasies and realities that constitute our worlds is no different from our denials of the differences in age, gender and culture that have shaped our personal and social histories. The wish of a child to deny and attack the adult capacities of its parents, in spite of its dependence on these very capacities for its own survival, is well-documented in Kleinian theory and practice, as are the ensuing guilt and paranoid feelings. Without this recognition, we are in danger of attacking the diversity of the intersubjective world whilst seemingly pursuing an ethical ideal of justice and freedom.

In my discussion of Habermas and Lyotard on rationality, I have tried to follow these three moments of contemporary philosophical discourse: the first, sometimes called epistemological is, in fact, the critique of scientific rationality; the second follows the linguistic turn and shifts the emphasis from science to language and to the intersubjective world of linguistic norms and actions by which we are bound; and finally, the third acknowledges the ethical dimension of the linguistic turn. The recognition of intersubjectivity exposes the need for respect and care for the other. It highlights the need for reflection on what the 'other' of reason or the 'other' in discourse could be, when different from myself or from what is already known. I follow these moves in the work of Habermas and Lyotard and, at every stage, I have tried to show in which ways a dialogue with psychoanalysis can contribute to the debate. The move from Freud to Klein emphasizes the need to move from a monological subject to the intersubjectivity of discourse. Ironically, Klein and her followers have been criticized for transforming the sexual theories of Freud into ethico–moral ones, whereas I believe it is their emphasis on loss, mourning, destructiveness, reparation, envy and gratitude, precisely the moral ideas, which brings a real contribution to the philosophical debate. The emphasis on the intersubjective meaning of our relationships to others and ourselves, an emphasis which does not depart from Freud's radical concept of the unconscious (as the id *and* the superego), makes the reading of Kleinian literature so rewarding.

The debate on rationality is fundamental to philosophy and the human sciences in general. What is at stake is not the defence of 'our' form of rationality as a disguised form of domination. In fact, this debate allows us to understand how the arguments used against reason are very much part of the modernist understanding of rationality. The disenchantment with reason makes for an idealization of the unknown and this idealization is potentially dangerous. It may also lead to a form of relativism which, whilst acknowledging the infinite variety of possibilities of interpretations, harbours a conservative core which denies and destroys the richness of meaning and interpretation. In this sense, the defence of reason must be approached as the search and care for the dimension of meaning and interpretation which is so central to our lives and which is so much under attack, particularly in the human sciences. Moreover, in our multicultural societies we must rethink our ideas of justice and respect for the 'other'. The growing emphasis on the small, the local and the diverse should not blind us to the idea of truth that implicitly guides the recognition of the diversity. We need, more than ever, an idea of reason that acknowledges and cares for this heterogeneity. The encounter with what reason is not and cannot be expands and enriches the project of modernity as the defence of rationality.

1

THE CRITIQUE OF REASON: HABERMAS AND LYOTARD

The big debate between the modernist and the postmodernist is a continuation of the old controversy about rationality. In general, the postmodernists claim that reason, being situated rationality, can no longer aspire to certainty. They also argue that the modern defenders of rationality can no longer maintain that truth is an objective idea. One of the possible corollaries of this position is the belief in reason as an instrument of control and domination. According to this view, Western rationality, claiming to speak in the name of truth, has, in fact, furthered totalitarianism and terror.

In the 1980s, Jean-François Lyotard made popular the idea that modernity is a reign of terror. In *The Postmodern Condition* he polemicized: 'We have paid a high enough price for the nostalgia of the whole and the one, for the reconciliation of the concept and the sensible, of the transparent and the communicable experience. Under the general demand for the slackening and for the appeasement, we can hear the mutterings of the desire *for a return of terror, for the realization of the fantasy to seize reality.*' [5]

Not surprisingly, the old Marxist idea that reason (and especially reason's highest achievement, science) can bring about enlightenment and emancipation, has been disputed. The old Marxist opposition between science and ideology, where the latter was the veil that covered the truth that science could reveal was, at best, forgotten and, at worst, became the symbol of the way Marxism provided the 'ideological' tools to legitimize political terror.

The belief in reason's capacity for enlarging our ideas of truth and freedom produced a tremendous concern with knowledge of the history of ideas. Philosophy as theory of knowledge has been one of the defining trends of modern philosophy, irrespective of the different ways of approaching the topic. Both the empiricist tradition, which questions the possibility of ever providing a rational grounding for knowledge, and the Cartesian view, which, whilst recognizing the doubts that assail rational knowledge, nevertheless seeks to provide a foundation to support it, are epistemological traditions, in the sense that their primary concern is with the grounds for knowledge.

The contradictions and problems of these projects have produced a variety of solutions and new questions. The main problem, however, springs from an approach to reason as a faculty that can be abstracted from its context. Reason as 'the mind', separated from both the body and the world of emotions, beliefs and values that surround it, cannot survive. In other words, rational knowledge, when abstracted from the individual subject's history and from the historical tradition which produces its self-understanding, is a myth that creates insoluble questions. In a sense, this dilemma is present in Descartes already, in so far as, in the *Meditations*, the only possible justification for rational knowledge is to be found in his (irrational) *belief* in God and the order He created. Reason in the end requires that which it is not, that which it is supposed to overcome and replace.

The reason the debate has become so interesting is the acknowledgement, in the rationalist–modernist camp, that reason is not a neutral instrument to achieve knowledge and truth. When Lyotard, the opponent of rationality, questions, in his famous book *The Postmodern Condition*, the role of knowledge in contemporary societies, it is Habermas, best known for his paper on the 'ideological' role played by technology and science in advanced capitalist societies, who answers him. Habermas's reply, 'Modernity: an Unfinished Project', was a speech given when he accepted the Adorno Prize.[6] It is as a disciple of Adorno and as belonging to the tradition of the Frankfurt School that Habermas speaks.

One of the main themes of this tradition was the Weberian recognition of modernity as an 'iron cage', where rationality, as means–end rationality, transforms thought and culture into meaningless operations aimed solely at success and efficiency. Thus, rationality becomes instrumental rationality and the realms of social, political and even artistic life are reduced to questions of the efficiency of experts in achieving certain ends. The dimension of meaning and the issues of quality of life and humanity have disappeared in a world dominated by criteria of efficiency and success, measured quantitatively, generally in financial terms. Weber had noted this transformation of time into units of production and how the division of the clock into quarters of an hour was to be considered a development of capitalism. He stressed that 'modern man in his professional life ... has no time, and even for instance – as Goethe was already doing in his *Wanderjahren* – measure[s] the extent of capitalist development by the fact that the clocks strike the quarter hours (as Sombart also says in his *Kapitalismus*'.[7] Even art, which for Adorno embodied the possibility of freedom, can become ruled by these criteria as, for instance, when music becomes controlled by the 'art' industry or the record companies. Marcuse, in his analysis of mass culture, described how the apparent choices of consumerist societies disguised the banality of what is in effect always the same. In *One-Dimensional Man,* he commented on the pseudo-choices the great number of American radio stations seemed to give, when, in fact, they did not, for as he moved from one station to the other, he discovered they were all the same. Still, it is as part of the tradition of the Frankfurt School and its critique of rationality that Habermas defends the modernist project of reason as emancipation.

Moreover, by using another dispute, the eighteenth century French literary *querelle* between the '*Anciens*' and the '*Modernes*' as the epitome of the formation of modernist consciousness, Habermas has been able to show how the identity of the modernists was formed against the idea of atemporal canons and rules of beauty. The *querelle* opposed, in the French Academy, the '*Anciens*', led by Boileau, to the '*Modernes*', led by Perrault. Boileau supported the classical rules of beauty and composition as laid down by tradition, whilst Perrault defended the invention and creation of new rules.[8] In other words, the modernist camp asserted that consciousness is formed in time and shaped by history. The modernist awareness of time does not deny the need for criteria and rules, rather, it reminds us that the need for criteria and rules follows from the questioning of the once absolute and atemporal canons of tradition. Habermas's retelling of the *querelle* as the epitome of the modernist consciousness shows that the historicity and contextuality of reason, generally associated with the postmodernist critique, is actually a central tenet of the modernist camp. Indeed, what Habermas is saying is that the acknowledgement of culture and history is not postmodernist challenges to rationality, but rather the greatest *rational* challenge that reason ever posed itself.

Another way of recognizing this challenge is to turn to Baudelaire's definition of modernity. In his essay 'The Painter of Modern Life', Baudelaire stresses that modernity is the ephemeral and the contingent. This definition, however, in Baudelaire's own words, is only a half, the other half being the eternal and the immutable: 'La modernité c'est le transitoire, le fugitif, le contingent, la moitié de l'art dont l'autre moitié est l'éternel et l'immuable'.[9] Indeed, the purpose of the *querelle* was not to deny the need for criteria, but to recognize the unavoidable striving for eternal ideas whilst emphasizing that these eternities are ephemeral. The eternal exists in the ephemeral, but the contingent longs and calls for the absolute.

Nevertheless, it was a certain response to this challenge that has crystallized in our minds as the typical modernist identity. This response has denied reason's fragility and limitations, and transformed the recognition of the ephemeral into an ode to the absolute. The best example of this fatal mistake for anyone who lived the hopes and disappointments of socialism has to be the work of Marx.

The relevance of Marxism has always been stressed in terms of its capacity for offering a scientific blueprint for the revolutionary transformation of the world. The fact that this revolution did not come about or, when it did, it disastrously eradicated the basic principles of freedom it sought to install, has produced deep suspicion of Marxism. It is important to stress, however, that what Marxism also purported to offer was an idea of freedom and transformation which, whilst eminently rational, acknowledged the irrational in it. Indeed, what Marx claimed, and which later Freud at an individual level also acknowledged, was that the consciousness of ourselves and of our times was determined by what he called 'objective relations' that pre-existed and shaped these ideas.

Without wanting to get into the nowadays scholastic discussion of the role of determination and freedom in the young and the old Marx,[10] it is important to underline the fact that Marx and the left in general were struggling with an idea of reason and knowledge that affirmed the possibility of freedom, but which, by the same token, also recognized the unknown dimension in itself. By realizing that unknown factors (call them class, call them economic relations, call them ideology) were part of reason, Marx was opening up an abyss where *critique itself* could be shaped by factors unknown.

One of the ways in which Marx and subsequent theorists attempted to solve the problem was by distancing themselves from the fundamental insight into the unknown dimensions of the process of critique. An arbitrary line could thereby be drawn between 'false', i.e. ideological knowledge, permeable to distortions and manipulations by the ruling classes, and 'true', i.e. scientific knowledge, which was protected from the world of uncertainties by the armour of Dialectic Materialism and the unquestionable guarantee of speaking in the name of the people.

Marx failed to pursue fully the idea that our understanding of the factors that distort knowledge could itself be shaped by unknown factors. His desire for a type of knowledge that would stand over and above these distortions is at the heart of the failures of Marxism. It also denies the radically new understanding of knowledge and reason that he himself proposed. The failure is, of course, central to the abuses of power 'in the name of the people' that happened when Marxist ideology came into power. In Latin America, it is part of the problems of some of the old left wing groups which, for years, struggled heroically underground. Now, as established legal parties, with real possibilities of power, the legacy of their certainty of possessing the truth is the main factor in their difficulties in participating in the creation of a democratic space.

The awareness of our time as a historical time is one of the central features of modernity. This awareness produces the modernist necessity of creating new criteria to ground modernity in itself. This task is impossible, in so far as an absolute grounding is ruled out by the very awareness of time brought about by modernity. If the stress is on the eternal, on the absolute, then the idea of time, and with it the recognition of history, disappears. Habermas has argued that Hegel, the philosopher who recognized the historicality of the new, modern age, in the end denied the very insight of the historicity of our times.[11] Indeed, when Hegel opts for an understanding of the Spirit as the Absolute, History becomes fate, and reason as self-reflection denies the problems it has created. If, however, on the other hand, the eternal disappears, the ephemeral becomes trivial and loses its meaning. It is important to bear this other side of the problem in mind. Indeed, we are so painfully aware of the mistakes of the quest for an absolute grounding that we are, if anything, more prone to err on the other side, the 'politically correct' postmodern relativism. The postmodern attack on modernity's longing for the absolute, for foundations and for criteria forgets that without this longing (which can never be fulfilled), language and art lose their significance. Modernity, as Baudelaire understood it, is the awareness of the present as a meeting-point between time and eternity.[12]

The problem that underlies this discussion is an old one, the theme of which has been played over in many variations, from Parmenides and Heraclitus to the Romantics and the Enlightenment. It is the problem created by an understanding of reason that acknowledges change and time, and which, in modern times, recognizes the irrational and the emotional which underlie reason's capacity for self-understanding.

Recently, this discussion has become popular as the opposition between relativism and objectivism.[13] This takes the form of questioning whether it is possible for reason to overcome the cultural, historical and individual differences created by our various forms of life. Reason becomes a possible language, relative to a certain context. The gap between the various contexts, which reason seeks to bridge, becomes the incommensurable abyss between untranslatable languages. Even the most basic moral and political norms, such as the right to life and freedom, become questionable ideas, relative to the Judeo–Christian tradition which has flourished in the West. Without such universal values, however, the possibility of justifying one's condemnation of the Holocaust, for example, disappears, as its perpetrators could claim that they saw it against their own background of values and norms, which did not recognize the humanity of Jews, Communists and other 'inferior' forms of life.

In our contemporary multicultural societies, we see the conflicts generated by this multiplicity of views. The option of a rational quest for universal values is a difficult one, generally associated with the most 'conservative' of ideals, the perpetuation of the domination of Western values. Any defence of the particular has to involve, somehow, however, the idea of the universal. The recognition of the differences in multicultural societies involves universal rights, irrespective of – or because of – each individual or cultural diversity. Without this recognition, the statement that all forms of life are relative to a certain context becomes itself of relative value, thus losing its point. The recognition of the inevitable universalistic dimension of political and moral values in general is not sufficient, however, to justify the validity of any specific right as, for instance, in the case of abortion and the conflict between the sometimes contradictory rights to life of the mother and those of the unborn child. General laws need to be seen against their specific backgrounds, where no answers are given once and for all. On the other hand, a radical relativism, which does not seek to universalize its own position, is also impossible to sustain.

The interest in following Habermas's defence of the rationality project lies precisely in the way in which he situates himself at the heart of a discussion of values. The modernity project as a defence of rationality was, from the very beginning of Habermas's work, an attempt to ground the idea of freedom. Habermas belongs to a tradition that sees in reason the possibility of emancipation, although he has also been careful to point out that this tradition does not imply a foundationalism in the strong sense of absolute groundings. In fact, one could say that to follow Habermas's philosophical development is to become acquainted with the necessary reworkings of the rational tradition, once it acknowledges that reason does not rule alone, outside its historical context.

Habermas, born in 1929, grew up in Nazi Germany, an experience that shaped the lives of most of the very influential thinkers of his time. The Frankfurt School group went into exile (Habermas became an assistant to Adorno in 1956), whilst Heidegger's thought and career were tainted by his sympathy for Nazism. Habermas has vigorously attacked the idea that one could excuse Heidegger's complicity as a weakness or as a naïvety that might beset geniuses, too busy with their own thoughts to be aware of worldly matters. For Habermas, thought is not outside reality; theory and practice, philosophy and politics are inextricably entangled. In fact, his critique of Heidegger argues that the latter's mystical understanding of Being created the space for the idealization of Nazism (Habermas, 1983, 1987b). For Habermas, therefore, philosophy is necessarily a critical theory of society, a reflection that should further and promote the ideal of emancipation from any form of domination.

Habermas's philosophical turns are not just exemplary of the main changes in modern philosophy. They also illustrate the road philosophy must take if it wants to remain politically committed to the ideas of freedom and emancipation. Thus, he moved from a concern with knowledge and epistemology – a concern too heavily involved with the notion of an autonomous subject of knowledge – to language and the intersubjective world of communication. This move has given him the background for developing a rational discussion of norms and values, his present discourse theory of ethics and law. The strength of Habermas does not lie in his style, heavy and sometimes too informed by disciplines of thought unknown to his readers; rather, it rests on his ability to learn from his opponents and to propose new readings of rationality that offer solutions to leading moral and political problems. Interestingly enough, the failures he faced in his three big projects, which I would call the epistemological, the linguistic and the moral, have similarities that might point to the weaknesses of these projects. In this sense, it is worth going into the details of his development, as they illuminate the pitfalls of a defence of rationality.

The interest in choosing Lyotard as the champion of postmodernity is more than the obvious argument of the authorship of a book that represents this critique (Lyotard, 1986). Indeed, the very ideas of an author and of representation have been strongly questioned by other philosophers such as Derrida (1977), who are likewise very suspicious of the claims of reason. The interest in the confrontation of Habermas and Lyotard lies in the fact that Lyotard too is looking for norms and working on the idea of political and moral judgement. On a number of occasions, Lyotard has provocatively turned the tables on his modernist opponent by implying that Auschwitz, the epitome of irrationality, the event which calls for general and universal outrage, is the best example of modernity.[14] Lyotard is, however, more of a champion of modernity than he would actually acknowledge, in the sense that his development, like Habermas's, points to the need for a reworking of the philosophical tradition. The move from a philosophy of the subject to the intersubjective world of language opens the way for a discussion of the meaning of ethics and judgement. Like Habermas, Lyotard moves from epistemology to language and from language to ethics, though in so doing he is always on the opposite side to Habermas, an opposition that complements and reinforces these moves rather than radically challenges them. Their interpretations of the need for such moves illuminate each other's positions in an extremely interesting way.

Habermas's and Lyotard's first move, from epistemology to language, follows the most important shift in twentieth century philosophy, namely the move from a philosophy centred on a revised Cartesian subject to a reflection that acknowledges the intersubjective world of beings and language. In other words, it is a move deeply inspired by Husserl's failure to provide a foundation for knowledge through phenomenology and by Heidegger's radical ontological critique of phenomenology.

Indeed, Husserl's phenomenology was the last grand attempt to ground knowledge and meaning in a transcendental subjectivity. His recognition, however, that the *cogito* was not a self-possessed subjectivity but a consciousness *of* other subjects and objects, moved the emphasis from the subject to the intentionality of the consciousness. As Heidegger later pointed out, Husserl's project of grounding knowledge in a subjectivity was undermined by phenomenology itself and its recognition that we – as beings, rather than as subjects of knowledge – are beings-in-the-world. The phenomenological insight into the intentionality of consciousness underlined this fundamental horizon of intersubjective relations. It stressed how our perceptions and thoughts are always thoughts and perceptions *of* something, and how objects and subjects are objects and subjects *for* a consciousness. If we take this idea seriously, we cannot go behind this horizon, a horizon that constitutes possible subjects and possible objects, and we have to accept that it is an ontological rather than an epistemological horizon. It then follows that the idea of a foundation of knowledge is dependent on the world that constitutes this knowledge with its requirement for grounding. The main feature of this world and of our being-in-the-world is language. In a sense, both Habermas and Lyotard have accepted this critique. Their different views as to its significance, however, leave them in radically opposed camps.

Habermas's major opus, *Knowledge and Human Interests*, can be said to be a struggle with and an acknowledgement of this hermeneutic tradition, that is, the recognition that we cannot go 'behind' or 'beyond' the horizon of language in which we are constituted as subjects of knowledge. His project was to create a critical science of society, a type of knowledge oriented towards the idea of emancipation. This project sought to rescue the idea of emancipation from a problematic materialist (Marxist) tradition and to criticize the idealist view of knowledge that sought to isolate science from the material, historical world which creates it. In those days, Habermas's main opponent was the positivist, who modelled rationality on the ideals of neutrality and objectivity inspired by the natural sciences. Against this, Habermas argued for the recognition of historically developed interests which shape our practices, including the scientific production of knowledge. This recognition has to acknowledge the scientistic (positivist) mistakes of Marxism, namely its view of itself as outside the crisis it wishes to depict. In order to question this view, Habermas stressed the hermeneutic insight that it is within language that we constitute ourselves as subjects of knowledge. We might, as natural scientists do, abstract ourselves from that world in order to 'get on' with our work, but science as a neutral objective description is itself a hermeneutic gambit, made possible by language, in language.

This is not the whole story, however. Indeed, for Habermas, if we were to stop here, as hermeneutics does, we could never produce a critique of language as distorted by domination. Language is itself a medium that develops historically and which can be, according to Habermas, a medium for power as much as for communication.[15] For Habermas, the collusion of Heidegger's hermeneutic philosophy with Nazism is unforgettable and unjustifiable. Indeed, as he has frequently argued, an approach to Being as that which escapes reason and mutual understanding, favours an uncritical and passive political and social existence.[16] The controversy surrounding Paul de Man's war record and Derrida's attempt to defend him is a further example of the difficulties facing a style of philosophy which rejects the idea of critique.[17] Habermas is particularly distrustful of the mysticism of Heidegger's ontology and its politico–philosophical implications. Whenever Habermas reads and acknowledges some important insights from Wittgenstein and the American Pragmatists, insights that have much in common with the hermeneutic tradition, he always reminds us of the need for norms and criteria for political judgement.

In the 1970s, these positions, hermeneutics and critical theory, came to a confrontation quite similar, in a way, to that between modernity and postmodernity. The analyses of these debates generally emphasized the strengths of contemporary hermeneutics.[18] This position, best represented by Gadamer's *Truth and Method*, recognized understanding and meaning as the fundamental dimensions of beings, but it also stressed the *historicality* of this understanding. And, unlike Habermas, this recognition of the historicality of understanding did not lead Gadamer to a search for universal norms and criteria. On the contrary, this recognition, for him, plunges us further into our horizons, into our own historical situatedness. Gadamer criticizes Habermas's idea of critique because it implies some sort of overcoming of tradition and history. For Gadamer, the critical theorist's critique of prejudices and traditions presupposes a horizon, in this case, the tradition of the Enlightenment, from where he speaks.[19] This is not to question his right or need to speak, but to question pointedly the assumed universality of this critique.

The fact that Habermas moved to a theory of language and communication seemed to constitute further proof of the triumph of hermeneutics and the priority it gave to language. The situation was, in fact, more complex. Habermas's move towards language was an acknowledgement that his conception of reason as self-reflection was still based on a solipsistic subjectivity. For Habermas, Gadamer's and Wittgenstein's greatest contribution was their view that understanding is *mutual* understanding. Thus, his linguistic turn was a move from a philosophy of the subject to a philosophy of intersubjectivity, a dialogical practice that takes place within a linguistic world. Nevertheless, within this framework, Habermas still wanted to affirm the role of critique and the possibility of working towards a rational idea of freedom. Against the hermeneutic conception of philosophy as interpretation, a rereading of meaning that in the end affirms the impossibility of universal values, Habermas sought to show how the mutual understanding that takes place between speakers every time language is spoken, implies the necessity of the idea of truth, of justice and of freedom. The move towards language helped Habermas to create the intersubjective framework necessary for a discourse theory of justice, his present moral and political philosophy.

The interest in discussing Lyotard's postmodernist position lies in the very different solutions Lyotard gave to these problems. As with Habermas, Lyotard's interest in phenomenology was mingled with a deep awareness of its political limitations. His first book, *La Phénoménologie*, was a militant appeal for a Marxist phenomenology, a current which Tran-Duc-Thao's *Phénoménologie et matérialisme dialectique* had initiated in France in the 1950s and which seemed, for a while, to overcome the dichotomy between the subjectivist, idealist positions of phenomenology and the objectivistic mistakes of Marxism. Although one is reminded of Habermas's introduction to *Knowledge and Human Interests*, which stated the same purpose, the difference later becomes markedly clear. The aftermath of *Knowledge and Human Interests* left Habermas with an ideal of critique as self-reflection, which was, ironically enough, too close to the problems of idealism he had sought to overcome. In contrast, the conclusion of *La Phénoménologie* revealed how profoundly enmeshed with the framework of Marxism Lyotard then was. Indeed, the concluding pages of *La Phénoménologie* were a militant appeal for a science of history to give a more solid base to the idealism of phenomenology. Lyotard was still working within a base/superstructure Marxist model. Undoubtedly, he also stressed the 'relative' autonomy of superstructural ideas, but he hoped to anchor these meanings to the material reality of the economic base. It is hard to remember that, in those days, the modernist Habermas was much closer to the idealism of phenomenology than he might wish to acknowledge today, and that the champion of postmodernity, Lyotard, was then a materialist crusader.

The fundamental points for Lyotard, then and throughout his œuvre, were politics and judgement. His wish to complement phenomenology with Marxism was based on his desire to develop a reflection on justice and political responsibility. In order to do so, however, Lyotard in the end had to abandon historical materialism and move closer to the recognition of the *meaning* of actions in history. Lyotard's reading of the hermeneutic tradition belongs to a historical and geographical context quite different from Habermas's. If, in Germany, hermeneutics meant Heidegger's political record, in occupied France the reading of the same tradition by Sartre's existentialism and Merleau-Ponty's phenomenology was quite opposite, in so far as they were explicitly concerned with the meaning of freedom and the need for political action. Lyotard, who recognized the major influence Merleau-Ponty exerted on his philosophical development, wanted to be able to tell the difference between the resistance fighter who kills and the Collaborator who kills. If these actions cannot be differentiated, they are all the same and have the same worth. Then there are no values and Auschwitz could be said to be the road to freedom and happiness.[20]

9

In this pursuit, Lyotard eventually had to abandon the Marxist framework which he had hoped would have provided such bedrock criteria. In fact, he became known for questioning the very search for criteria as one of the evils of modern philosophy.[21] Still, it was not phenomenology that exploded Lyotard's Marxist framework, rather, it was his wish to understand history and political judgements which, in the end, brought him back to language for his critique of rationality. Lyotard's courageous and perceptive critique of established left wing politics in France and the Soviet Union in the 1950s led to a growing dissatisfaction with Marxism. In the end, Lyotard's political critique of totalitarianism, as in, for instance, his writings in the journal *Socialisme et Barbarie*,[22] culminated in the abandonment of grand theories and in a philosophical return to language.

In *Discours, Figure* Lyotard explored the ways in which philosophy reduced language to its descriptive use, an imbalance that has privileged philosophy as a discourse on knowledge. Language as rhetoric, as *figure*, is also the capacity for expressing feelings, and the possibility of creating worlds that can be later characterized by language as *discours*. At the end of the book, Lyotard tried to find ways to innovate and blend these two modes, in an attempt to reintroduce the dimension of rhetoric to philosophy. In his later development, however, he took a more radical approach. For Lyotard, reason and the discursive capacity of language became the evils responsible for the domestication and stifling of creativity, whilst the dimension of rhetoric, epitomized by artistic expression, symbolized that which reason tries by all means to oppress and repress, that which, by his own definition, cannot be known: the 'other' of reason.

In taking this path, Lyotard lost his voice, so to speak. His critique of reason as discourse led him to a suspicion of all theories, and to an idealization of the 'other' of reason that could only contradict his own philosophical excursions (even as *figures*). Interestingly enough, this idealization took the revealing form of an enchantment with the body. It was as if the only way to talk and think about that which is not rational would have to be the presentation of the material reality of desire, of libidinal instinctual impulses, which would amount to a paradoxical return to a crude form of positivism.[23] Although Lyotard later regained the power and purpose of his critique through his old political concern with judgement and justice, it is worthwhile considering for a moment this understanding of the 'other' of reason, and what role it played in both Habermas's and Lyotard's projects. For what is at stake in the modernity/postmodernity discussions is not just an understanding of reason as differentiated capacities that cannot be reduced to scientific discourse. Nor, as we have said, is the contrast between the two views to be drawn on the basis of the recognition of reason as shared rationality. The great difference between these two positions lies not in their understanding of what reason is not, but of what is, nevertheless, intrinsic to it.

Earlier we mentioned Marx, as a writer who struggled with this understanding of ourselves as constituted by unknown factors, and how the radicality of this insight was denied by the Marxist ideal of a *science* of history (Dialectic Materialism). Freud produced a richer understanding of that which is not known — the unconscious — but which, nevertheless, makes knowledge, including psycho-analytical knowledge, possible. Habermas's and Lyotard's responses to Freud illuminate how difficult it is for *both* authors to think this 'other' of reason. Their difficulties reveal the problems that underlie the modern and postmodern conceptions of rationality. These problems set limits to both Lyotard's and Habermas's philosophical gestures towards language and ethics.

Lyotard idealizes the unknown to the point where he is torn between a eulogy of fragmentation and a crude return to the empirical reality of 'the body' (desire). In so doing, he distances himself from Freud's understanding of the unconscious and of the meaning of unconscious fantasies. Freud's idea of unconscious fantasies emphasized the psychic reality of unconscious structures that shape our perceptions and understanding.[24] Lyotard's attacks on Freudian orthodoxy are, in fact, aimed at psychoanalysis as a *rational* investigation. What Lyotard cannot accept is the idea of a knowledge of that which is not directly available to consciousness but which, nevertheless, makes knowledge possible.

Habermas's approach is totally different, but he also fails to accept the radicality of Freud's idea of the unconscious and cannot, therefore, incorporate it in his understanding of rationality. His initial acceptance of Freud was not so much based on Freud's theory of the mind as on the possibility of creating a model for the critical sciences. Habermas's critique of knowledge sought to overcome the limitations of both the natural and the human sciences. Psychoanalysis for Habermas was an example of a type of knowledge that overcame the positivism of the natural sciences (psychoanalysis understood that even physical symptoms have meaning), whilst seeking to go beyond the lack of theoretical explanations associated with the hermeneutic model.

Habermas's classification of knowledge was not based on the attributes of the objects of enquiry (the natural or the human sciences); rather, his critique of positivism made a point of showing how knowledge was constituted around interests which are basic to the historical survival of the species. The *empirical–analytic* sciences constituted one possible form of knowledge, organized around the interest in mastering and controlling objectified processes, natural or social, following the mode of instrumental action. Such sciences are nomological, that is, they rely on general laws and explanations that aim at successful prediction and control. Habermas showed how this type of knowledge follows the mode of action of labour as the use of tools for a certain end. The human species is not solely a tool-making animal, however, as some Marxists, in the pursuit of 'scientificity', unfortunately assumed. As Marx himself pointed out, human beings interact; they engage socially. In fact, the precondition for using tools is a social capability, which is dependent on communicative interaction, on meaning and on understanding. Therefore Habermas included a second type of knowledge in his classification, the *historico-hermeneutic* sciences, constituted around the interest in securing and expanding the intersubjectivity of partners in communication.

Historico-hermeneutic knowledge produces an understanding of the world of shared norms, values and meaning. In the empirical-analytic sciences, language is used mainly monologically, as a tool for producing explanations with predictive power, without any regard for possible communicative partners. In the historico-hermeneutic world, language involves dialogue and the concept of partners in communication. Not surprisingly, this type of knowledge is, above all, interested in the categories of meaning and interpretation, and does not rely on explanations and law-like hypotheses with predictive powers. As we mentioned before, the communicative experience cannot be approached by the empirical-analytic sciences, in so far as communication cannot be reduced to the world of instrumental actions, geared towards the successful control and mastery of objects. The life-world of values and meanings shows how instrumental action is a possible form of action, by no means the only one open to us, and one which, in fact, presupposes the communicative world.

Habermas, however, wanted to go further,. For him, the hermeneutic standpoint cannot show how language can be distorted y power. Of course, the idea of a distorted communication is questioned by both contemporary hermeneutics and postmodernists. Gadamer replied to Habermas that the idea of critique as providing universal norms for truth, justice and freedom, forgets that we cannot get outside history and language. The Enlightenment ideal of overcoming prejudices and ignorance is formed within – and not outside – a horizon of understanding. Habermas nevertheless wanted to maintain this idea of critique. To this end, in his epistemological project, he posited a third type of science, different from the empirical-analytic and the historico-hermeneutic ones, and constituted around a third interest of the species, namely the interest in emancipation. Psychoanalysis was the best example of such a science.

Psychoanalysis for Habermas was a reflection on meaning and interpretation which, unlike hermeneutics, also resorted to strong theoretical assumptions and explanations. It combined hermeneutic understanding with causal explanations. In fact, Habermas stressed how the possibility of understanding the meaning of a distorted communication in the analytical setting required the analyst to interweave his understanding with an explanation of the origins of the distortion. This 'depth', or 'explanatory' hermeneutics produces a practical transformation, a liberation from internal distortions that illustrates the possibility of reason (critical theory) as emancipation.[25]

Thus, it is as a model for the critical sciences that psychoanalysis matters for Habermas. In *Knowledge and Human Interests*, he stressed how important it was for Freud to part (though never fully) with his ideal of a natural science of the psyche. What was fundamental was that symptoms had a meaning, even when this meaning had been lost to the patient. For Habermas, psychoanalysis comes of age when Freud realizes that it is not hypnosis, that is, that it requires more than the liberation of some mental energy: it requires a *self-understanding* of the symptom. Psychoanalysis is emancipatory when it produces an understanding that restores a meaning that had previously been lost.

Psychoanalysis as an example of critical science showed the dead end into which the epistemological project had led Habermas. In *Knowledge and Human*

Interests, the approach to reason as forms of knowledge made it quite difficult to assert the idea of reason as emancipation. Indeed, the idea of emancipation remained too close to an ideal of self-reflection as a knowledge separate from the intersubjective world that gave rise to it. As Dallmayr (1972) pointed out at the time, the idea of emancipation as knowledge created the paradox of an avant-garde of critical scientists, although this elite of intellectuals would have had the task of eliminating the gap between theory and practice, between pure and practical reason.

Habermas's approach to psychoanalysis as a critical science overemphasized the dimension of change made possible by psychoanalytical *knowledge*. Habermas was over-privileging the role of knowledge in bringing about change, though, to be fair, he was also stressing that this knowledge is part of an interaction which involves other dimensions of human relations, and this is particularly relevant in the case of psychoanalytical dialogue. This approach, in the end, exposed the limits of a conception of knowledge as *self*-reflection. Indeed, psychoanalysis as emancipation is not the knowledge possessed by the analyst, as a reflection of the subject, on his own. Contrary to some popular criticism of psychoanalysis, insight is not the imposition on the patient of the analyst's *Weltanschauung*. Psychoanalysis reveals the necessary intersubjective world of dialogue for insight to take place. The limitations of Habermas's epistemological project, too centred still on an idea of emancipation as self-reflection, were made clear by his own account of psychoanalysis as a critical science, that is, as a practice which requires a dialogue, an interaction.

Through Freud, Habermas acknowledged the intersubjective world which constitutes human rationality and makes emancipation possible. The radical psychoanalytical idea of the unconscious, however, so crucial to Freud, was more difficult for him to accept. Habermas over-emphasized the dimension of intersubjective relations that can be known to the detriment of that which is never fully known. It is therefore not surprising to note that Habermas has lost interest in Freud and in psychoanalytical theory, feeling much more at home in the hands of Piaget. Piaget, as we know, upholds an idea of rational development which privileges cognition over the emotional, a position that has been widely criticized precisely for this shortcoming.[26] The much richer understanding of Freud which reveals the complex web of emotional and intellectual interaction for understanding to come about has been left behind. This difficulty with the unconscious marks and limits Habermas's understanding of rationality. It also restricts and weakens his move to a communicative theory of action and to his discourse on ethics.

Lyotard's reading of Freud, on the other hand, praises the freedom of libidinal drives – the 'other' of reason – as an alternative to the oppression of knowledge and rationality. His writings of the time are almost embarrassing. They read as a naïve, enchanted ode to the body. They are also quite revealing. *Economie libidinale* opens with the carving up of a body, starting with the skin and then proceeding to reveal the various layers of meaningless disjointed pieces, with particular emphasis on lips and labia that open to other orifices or parts that again lead to other parts.[27] The strangely detached procedure is quite aseptic; the reader is not invited to fear or to step back in disgust. The reader is, in fact, invited to do something that is nothing more than a parody of so-called objective, scientific practice: the reader is invited to observe this cutting down of a body as if taking part in a Dionysian feast: 'Do the work that the sun does when you sunbathe, the job that pot does.' This praise of cutting, splitting and fragmentation as an alternative to rational discourse is an utter failure. The invitation to look, to cut into a body and to stare at its fragmented pieces does not succeed in bringing about the orgiastic effect it is supposed to induce. The detached anatomical exercise is too close to scientific analysis to be an alternative to it. It is a celebration of power rather than an alternative to it.

In fact, *Economie libidinale* unwittingly reveals that a critique of reason cannot be a celebration of the body and its fragmentation. An alternative to scientific rationality has to start with our capacity for understanding and integrating the various meanings of such fantasies (Habermas's question of what makes communication possible). As a celebration of pure desire, *Economie libidinale* illustrates how indebted to the model of knowledge as domination Lyotard's alternative still is. As a critique of reason, it helps to show how meaningless our actions become once we try to ground them in an ultimate reality: a body, in contra-distinction to a mind, or a context, in contra-distinction to the interaction that takes place in that context. The ideas of a 'body' or of a 'context' become hypostatized as an ultimate truth, and we return to a crude empiricism (the 'realities' of a specific cultural/historical/personal context, or the body), thus leaving no intelligible space for the role of meaning. The insight into language as having an infinity of possible meanings is extremely important in order to avoid a naïve empiricist view of objective reality as the foundation of meaning. But the flight into the multiplicity of meanings can deny the real puzzle we confront every time we engage in communication. The real question is: *Given the multiplicity of meanings, how do we explain even a partial mutual understanding?* If we deny that communication does take place, we are left with an idealization of madness which interchanges with a celebration of the fragmented body as the only possible real.

Lyotard's reading of Freud located the alternative to rational knowledge in primary instinctual processes. This is a particular reading of Freud, undoubtedly supported by Freud's own dream of a biological science of the psyche, which we shall discuss later on. Lyotard's disappointment with science in terms of the power and domination implicit in its theory and practice, led him to a celebration of the unconscious as pure libidinal instinct. This radical position implied a deep distrust of all theories, including psychoanalysis. Psychoanalytical practice then becomes not an opportunity for emancipation but an exercise in oppression and repression of desire, in the name of what he saw as a merely defensive formation, namely the self as the embodiment of rationality.

Needless to say, this is not what Freud had in mind. In his recognition that the subject is not the master of his or her own house, Freud still profoundly believed in the value and the possibility of rational enquiry. Although psychoanalysis is a form of knowledge which is itself permeated by unconscious processes (there is no thought which somehow is not part of the fuller emotional life which involves the unconscious), this does not mean that psychoanalysis is not possible *qua* rational reflection. After all, Freud famously hoped that where id was ego should be. This is a clear warning that reason should not be reduced to the unconscious. On the other hand, we should also be careful and remember that a transformation has taken place in this case. It is not the unanalyzed ego, who narcissistically and omnipotently denies the existence of the id which 'shall be' in its place, but the ego that has been humbled by the recognition that it is not the only psychic instance. Reason cannot and should not be reduced to the unconscious and nor should we understand the quest for reason as the denial and domination of that which it is not. Although psychoanalysis seeks to understand the meaning of a complex mental object that has, undoubtedly, a biological stratum, it cannot be reduced to it, as Lyotard dangerously does. As mentioned before, Habermas stresses that psychoanalysis started when Freud abandoned hypnosis as the favoured method for the exploration of the psyche.[28] The move away from hypnosis is the recognition of the hermeneutic dimension of psychic life: fantasies have meaning as well as a somatic substratum. If we do not recognize this, we run the risk of transforming the meaning we reveal in psychoanalytical dialogue into an empirical objectivity.[29]

Freud is the author who most challenged what could be called modernity's narcissism, that is, an omnipotent belief in reason, at least in our capacity for consciously understanding ourselves. After all, as he himself saw it, he delivered a crucial blow to our understanding of our rational capabilities, comparable with the shock of Copernicus' demotion of the earth as the centre of the universe and of Darwin's sobering questioning the primacy of man at the centre of nature. Freud recognized that we were no longer 'masters in our own houses', that there were emotional forces and a personal history that shaped and distorted our conscious understanding of ourselves. In other words, Freud recognized the particularly postmodern insight that there is an 'other' to reason that defines what reason is – even communicative reason.

Unlike the postmodern critic, however, for Freud the acknowledgement of the unconscious is the starting-point of an eminently rational (and modernist) endeavour: psychoanalysis. It is in the name of autonomy and science that Freud engages in the understanding of unconscious meaning: 'Where id was, ego shall be'. This is, however, a different ego and a different reason. From now on, the subject must know that his unconscious life, shaped by his personal intersubjective history, epitomized by his relationship to his parents and its correlate world of affects and fantasies, colours his perception of himself and others. There will never be a thorough 'chimney sweeping' as the first patients in analysis hoped for. We cannot 'clear out' the unconscious for, without it, conscious thought cannot exist. We can hope to achieve, however, a changed understanding of ourselves, one that acknowledges the role of other subjects and non-rational elements in what we used to think of as solely 'ours'. This acknowledgement does not threaten the status of psychoanalysis as a rational enquiry. Indeed, for Freud, psychoanalysis is inaugurated in the name of reason, for the sake of knowledge as the foundation of happiness and autonomy. What has changed in the process is our idea of reason and knowledge as monological, that is, narcissistic and omnipotent.

Habermas's main difficulty lies precisely in understanding what this knowledge is and accepting its limits. Psychoanalytical work, which encompasses the cognitive and the emotional is, for Habermas, mainly cognitive. Thus, he says that '[analytic knowledge] is critique in the sense that the analytic power to dissolve dogmatic attitudes inheres in analytic insight. Critique *terminates* in a transformation of the affective–motivational basis, just as it begins with its need for practical transformation.'.[30]

This is a very different point from Freud's who recognized the need for working through, in the transference, the resistances of the patient. In other words, for Freud, the analytical work does not *terminate* in a transformation of the emotional base through knowledge; rather, there is a need for an emotional rearrangement which will enable a non-defensive intellectual understanding. In his paper 'Remembering, Repeating and Working Through', Freud argues that, for a successful treatment, the analyst must 'allow the patient time to become conversant with this resistance that is *unknown* to him ('unbekannten'), to work through it, to overcome it, by continuing, in defiance of it, the analytic work according to the fundamental rule of analysis…'. This is such a novel idea that Strachey, who translated the paper, tried to 'clarify' it by translating it as 'resistance with which he has now become acquainted'. For Strachey this seemed to make 'good sense', though he was careful to include a note saying that Freud preferred 'unbekannten'.[31]

Although Habermas's critique of Marxism was directed precisely at the dangers of a critique that saw itself as outside its own scope, he found it difficult to understand the centrality of this reflexive notion for Freud. Of course, he stressed the positivist dangers of Freudianism, with its dreams of a natural science of the psyche. But the more subtle positivist danger, which Freud avoided, of seeing reason (or analysis) as a look that avoids its own gaze, is still present in Habermas's understanding of psychoanalysis.

The practice of psychoanalysis, probably by the very nature of its intersubjective setting, forced the analysts to become aware of this reflexivity. Indeed, psychoanalysis, and more particularly object–relations theory, understood the importance of the unconscious, not just on the patient's side, but on the analyst's as well. That meant that they could look at the unconscious as creating problems for thinking but also as enabling understanding.

Psychoanalysis is possible because of the transference, that is, because of the actualisation, in the analytic setting, of the patient's unconscious wishes. Thus, the powerful feelings of Anna O. for Breuer were understood by Freud not to be a hindrance but the central psychoanalytical material: the transference. These feelings were so strong that Anna O. imagined herself to be pregnant by Breuer, a situation that made him abandon all interest in psychoanalysis and flee to a second honeymoon with his wife, in order to recover from such a traumatic experience. More recently, psychoanalysis has developed an understanding of the *counter*-transference, that is, of the role of the analyst's unconscious. Nowadays, in order to understand Anna O., analysts would also be asking themselves about the unconscious wishes of Breuer, which produced such an unbearable state of panic that he had to terminate all contact with Anna O., and with psychoanalysis. In other words, analysts now recognize, as a basic tool of their trade, the role of the countertransference, that is, how the analyst's conscious and unconscious fantasies can be mobilized by communication with the patient. Psychoanalysis shows how the look directed at the patient's material comes from within the analyst's own conscious and unconscious mental life. To wish for an interpretation that would be devoid of such traces would be to deprive the analyst of what is now recognized as a fundamental tool for interpretation, namely the reflection on what sort of responses are produced by a certain material.

The recognition of the role of the countertransference is a central tenet of the Kleinian and the Independent schools of psychoanalysis which we shall discuss later on.[32] The recognition of the role of the countertransference was a considerable departure from Freudian orthodoxy. After all, Freud had advised analysts to follow the model of the surgeon 'who puts aside his own feelings, even his human sympathy, and concentrates his mental forces on the single aim of performing the operation as skilfully as possible'.[33]

This acknowledgement is not simple. There is a well-known anecdote amongst Kleinians that illustrates the dangers of this way of thinking. An analyst under supervision with Mrs Klein complained that her patient X elicited very intense feelings of disorientation and confusion in her, to which Mrs Klein replied that *the analyst* was the confused and disoriented one, not the patient.[34] It takes, however, the formidable personality of a Mrs Klein to be unfazed by the challenge the countertransference sets to any naïve conception of truth. As we postmodern beings know, the experience of intersubjectivity and reflexivity leads generally to a radical questioning of truth and knowledge.

Habermas has always wanted to produce a critical science which would go beyond the positivist misconception of the natural sciences. Nevertheless, the full acknowledgement that reason includes in itself that which is not known – a major argument in Habermas's attack on positivism – has so far eluded him, probably for fear of the mysticism, relativism and lack of political responsibility that have traditionally accompanied such a view. Habermas has thus abandoned to the postmodern that which he should never have done, namely reason as constituted by that which is not known. Psychoanalysis is a modernist science precisely because it acknowledges the 'other' of reason as part of reason, whilst still searching for a rational understanding of ourselves that could lead to autonomy and freedom.

Habermas's and Lyotard's views on Freud illustrate the shortcomings of their approach to rationality. Habermas's fear of the unconscious makes him identify with an ideal of rationality that can come dangerously close to the ideas of his old foe, positivism. This will become even clearer in the next chapter, as we look at his linguistic turn. On the other hand, Lyotard's idealization of the unconscious makes him suspicious of all theories and forms of knowledge as defensive, repressive formations. This position leaves him with little space for a reflection on judgement. Moreover, this idealization of fragmentation generally subsumes an empirical reality (the body, or in the case of language, the specific linguistic competences as irreconcilable 'savoirs-faire'). This is a dangerous trend, as it might legitimize that which it was meant to criticize: postmodern, technologically-oriented societies/knowledge. I believe that a return to psychoanalysis could be a salutary reminder of the unknown in communicative rationality, thus providing important insights into a discourse theory of ethics and into a reflection on judgement.

Contemporary developments in psychoanalysis, known as object–relations theory, have moved away from an economic model of the psyche, exemplary of Freud's reluctance to move away from the natural sciences. The economic point of view understands psychical processes in terms of the increase/decrease of quantities of instinctual energy that has been circulated and distributed.[35] Object–relations theories emphasize the unconscious fantasies that are the mental counterparts of the biological instincts. For some purists, psychoanalysis has lost its bearings, as it deals less with sexuality and more with what would normally be termed moral concerns, namely envy and gratitude, guilt and reparation, autonomy and responsibility.

Object–relations theories turned away from the model of instinctual economy mainly because of their emphasis on relations between subjects (which can be part-objects, such as the breast) and the fantasies that shape these relations. The specific interest in the complex interrelationship of the transference and the countertransference has shown the various devices we use to maintain our psychic equilibrium, and how these devices include specific ways of relating to or turning away from other objects. Thus, rather than a return to an original sexual trauma, and the correlate release of repressed memories which was part of the economic/energetic model, Kleinian analysts try to understand how, in the here and now of the transference, we recreate our ways of coping with our earlier history of relations with others.

For Kleinians, there are two basic configurations of the mental world, and these two basic positions are exemplary of two ways of dealing with intersubjective reality. In the paranoid–schizoid position, the world is split in two: the good and the bad objects, the bad ones being excluded, denied, destroyed or projected outside. Anxiety, which is generally intense, is of a persecutory type, due to the attacks on the object. In the depressive position, there is an attempt to apprehend the object more as a whole, good and bad. This position seeks to reintegrate parts of oneself which had been split off and denied. The depressive position, which in spite of its name is actually the position where we are freer from our more destructive aspects, is the recognition of the others that form our world, of how dependent I am, for my own happiness, on the endurance and existence of others. The paranoid position is the destructive denial of the existence of the world of intersubjective relations, and the manic attempt to restore the fiction of an isolated and omnipotent subject

18

(myself, all good), who sees the other as a different sort of being (bad and completely distinct from my regal self).

The analysis of the transference and the countertransference explores precisely the movement between these positions. It shows how the emotions and thoughts that the patient cannot express or possess are 'put into' (projected onto) the analyst. We can then start to understand what Strachey found so bewildering, namely the unknown with which the patient must familiarize himself in order to know. The idea of autonomy gains a new meaning with the recognition of the possibility of reintegrating parts of ourselves and our minds that have caused unbearable conflict and have had to be split off. This also means that we eventually have to face the loss of an ideal, conflict-free existence, both within ourselves and in the external world. But it means too that we can start to grasp what a truly intersubjective world we live in, and how the indeterminate and ever shifting barriers of I and Thou, We and They can be constructed to serve specific purposes, manic or defensive. The very crucial point of the depressive position is that it shows how fundamental to our autonomy and happiness is a sense of owning up to our objects (that is, the subjects we relate to) and to our attacks on them.

This type of analysis is radically opposed to the cognitive psychology of Piaget, in that it has developed a theory of thinking and processes of symbolization which link the capacity for abstract thought with the unconscious world of fantasies and anxieties. The work of Klein, Bion and Segal explore the ways in which thinking is not-thinking, that is, the ways in which one can refuse to see and turn away from understanding and insight. It shows how the 'skin' of our bodies and the boundaries of our minds are constructed through an interchange of projections and introjections. This awareness reveals ourselves as pertaining to a social world and responsible for our internal and external objects (our relations to other subjects), in ways that we do not necessarily know.

These contemporary developments in psychoanalysis can help us to see the limitations of Habermas's and Lyotard's critiques of epistemology and the philosophy of the subject. Indeed, because the concept of the unconscious and the psychoanalytical model are so central to their critiques of subjectivity and science, it is quite revealing to see what they fail to acknowledge fully in Freud. In Lyotard's case, the radicality of his approach to the unconscious as the 'other' of reason forces him to negate any formulation of this 'other', as it would be a 'domestication', a betrayal of the 'otherness' of the unknown. This position not only forces him into a dead end where the unconscious becomes the (somatic) repository of instinctual energies, but it also strangely leads him away from an understanding of the 'other' as other than oneself. Indeed, the radical critique of the isolated autonomous Cartesian subject as belonging to a world of intersubjective relations cannot come about here, as Lyotard's 'other' is not another person, but a radically different entity, forever unknown. The 'other' is also another person, however, (and Habermas's theory of communicative action leads our thoughts in this direction), with whom I interact and whose presence in fact, as Sartre reminds us, forces me to look at myself as an 'other' for the 'other' who is also an 'I'. Sartre recognized with horror this fundamental dimension of humanity, as for him this was an attack on freedom. Still, what was seen by Sartre as a terrific blow is, in fact, according to Kleinian analysis, the very possibility of our sanity, a recognition of belonging to a world of other subjects who can never fulfil their Sartrean dream of omnipotent autonomy. In Lyotard's case, the 'other' becomes solely the unknown and not the face of the 'other', with whom and to whom I relate, and therefore we are back to a world of isolated subjectivities who possess, no doubt, an internal unknown territory, one which strangely reminds us of a naturalistic landscape of instinctual energy. Lyotard's move to language is meant to take him away from this instinctual dead end, and allow him into an intersubjective world where the question of judgement must inevitably be asked. Thus, the idea of an 'other' of reason becomes an ethical question, one that must acknowledge from the start the recognition of the 'other' also as another person.

As for Habermas, the recognition of the unconscious has been progressively abandoned, to the point where it hardly merits a mention in his more recent writings, in spite of its being so fundamental to the idea of emancipation from unknown distortions of power. The recognition of the unconscious did lead Habermas to abandon the notion of the isolated subject. For Habermas, psychoanalysis, the best example of a critical science, revealed that an emancipatory reflection could only come about through dialogue. But the idea of the unconscious as unknown, as that which resists, sometimes violently, being known, was and is anathema to him. Not surprisingly, as we saw, for Habermas the understanding of what is to be gained through analysis is mainly a cognitive achievement, one that never fully acknowledges the whole emotional and personal transformation necessary for such cognitive insights to take place. That, of course, is a misunderstanding of Freud's reworking of what insight and knowledge can become when informed by the unconscious, and it leaves Habermas with a formal and abstract understanding of rationality.

Moreover, this misunderstanding has repercussions on his theory of communicative action. Habermas's central contention in his move to language is that the ideals of truth and justice can be recovered if we approach reason as intersubjective, communicative reason. The ideas of dialogue and the agreement to be reached through dialogue are therefore fundamental. But the other central insight which derives from the unconscious is that this 'other' that ego is not, is also the object it assimilates. In other words, the idea of transference, which the Kleinians extended to the countertransference, is more than the need for a partner for reflection and communication to take place. It is the recognition of the power of the self to incorporate, through introjections and projections, the 'other' as the same, or to use the 'other' as a repository of its own unwanted or unbearable parts. This, of course, makes the idea of dialogue much more problematic, as the boundaries between self and others become much more fluid. The idea of the 'other' as the unknown – and not merely as that which will be known through rational dialogue – is also the recognition of the emotional impact of what we cannot own and control. Without an understanding of how violently we can negate the nonidentical, we cannot assume, even as an idea, the possibility of dialogue between selves. As Jessica Benjamin points out, an intersubjective theory must 'pose the question of how and whether the self can actually achieve a relationship to an outside 'other' without, through identification, assimilating and being assimilated by it.'[36]

Habermas's move towards language is a recognition of the limitations of the epistemological project, that is, of reason as knowledge. But without an understanding of rationality which fully acknowledges that which is not conscious and explores the ways in which thinking is shaped by emotional life, the problems of the philosophy of the subject, namely its restricted self-definition (as male, or white, or Western) and its empty formalism, will continue to haunt Habermas's emancipatory project. The broader understanding of rationality to be gained from psychoanalysis is not restricted to self-understanding; it also shows how a reflection upon oneself reveals the social world in which we exist. Instead of the mystical silence of hermeneutics, the acknowledgement of the unknown in reason, via psychoanalytical thinking, leads to a recognition that the pursuit of autonomy and happiness is indissociable from the struggle for justice and freedom in the social world.

2

HABERMAS'S LINGUISTIC TURN

The predominant trait of twentieth century philosophy is the move towards language. Language is no longer thought of as a neutral medium for knowledge, nor as a tool that we use to describe and decode the world. Language shapes our knowledge of ourselves and of the worlds we live in. Habermas and Lyotard both accepted that the project of grounding truth and ethics on science and knowledge produced more problems than it solved. Their acceptance of the need to take the linguistic road, however, meant a different project for each of them.

For Lyotard, the linguistic turn meant the recognition that we must surpass our 'humanist' tradition, too close to the Enlightenment project of overcoming prejudice and ignorance through knowledge. He clearly states in *The Differend* that his purpose is to 'refute the prejudice anchored in the reader by centuries of humanism and of "human sciences" that there is "man", that there is "language", that the former makes use of the latter for his own ends, and that if he does not succeed in attaining these ends, it is for want of good control over language "by means" of a "better" language'.[37] The search for knowledge and truth – what Lyotard calls 'grand narratives' – can undermine the fundamental hermeneutic recognition that a theory of knowledge is only possible in language and through language. This is not language created by 'man'. This is the recognition that man is created by our intersubjective linguistic world.

The same linguistic turn, however, meant the opposite to Habermas. For Habermas, it meant the affirmation of the modernist project of the Enlightenment, now no longer based on an isolated subjectivity, but on the intersubjectivity of language. For Habermas, the recognition of the limitations of the epistemological project, too enmeshed with the idea of philosophy as self-reflection, only reaffirms the need for an intersubjective reflection on truth and justice, thus asserting the need for more, rather than less, philosophical theory.

From the start their projects seemed diametrically opposed. Lyotard's main attack on Habermas concentrated on the latter's approach to language as *consensus,* an 'outmoded and suspect value'.[38] Nevertheless, although he questioned Habermas's project, Lyotard also sought to reclaim, on behalf of the postmodernist camp, the reflection on justice which had traditionally been associated with the humanist tradition. As he put it, 'justice is neither outmoded nor suspect'.[39] It is worth trying to understand what Habermas means by consensus, in order to see if Lyotard's alternative view of language as consisting of heteromorphous, irreconcilable language games is a more adequate way of producing an idea and a practice of justice.

Habermas's linguistic turn does start with a surprising – and undoubtedly controversial – way of looking at language. Time and again he has clearly stated his purpose of seeking the conditions of possibility of understanding, as he thinks that 'all other forms of social action – for example, conflict, competition, strategic action in general – are *derivatives* of action oriented towards reaching understanding'.[40]

This type of transcendental reflection, which assumes that language is, essentially, directed towards understanding, seems to be inadequate for various reasons. We seem to be back to the classical epistemological project, with its search for the essential rules (or grounds) of language. Implied by this view is the idea that language has an essence or a deep structure from which other forms of communication or performance are derived. The knowledge of this deeper structure – the universal conditions of possibility of understanding – would provide the conditions of possibility of all language games. This view of language is questionable on the grounds of the linguistic turn itself, which, influenced by Wittgenstein, sought to overcome this dream of a linguistic analysis.[41]

Wittgenstein's approach to language as language games was a strategy devised to affirm the infinite creativity and diversity of language, in order to refute the idea that language had an essence. This is how he writes about language games: 'I am saying that these phenomena have no one thing in common which makes us use the same word for all – but that they are related to one another in many different ways.'.[42] They share a 'family resemblance', that is, rather than having a common trait or essence, each language game has ways of relating to others, and those others in turn to yet others. Indeed, family members resemble each other in surprisingly creative ways, sometimes even (but not necessarily) sharing the same nose. Language has no deeply buried essence which the philosopher must unveil or discover. Philosophy must turn away from this wish to give language its ultimate foundation.[43]

Habermas himself seemed to accept this approach to language, when he praised Wittgenstein's view of language as consisting of language games in his 'Sprachspiel, Intention und Bedeutung' and criticized Chomsky's notion of competence in 'Towards a Theory of Communicative Competence'.[44] In fact, Habermas felt much closer to Chomsky's project than to Wittgenstein's, as his initial choice of name for his linguistic turn – a theory of communicative competence – made clear.

Chomsky started from two main features of language. The first one is the *creativity* of the speakers, that is, the ability of every competent speaker to form an infinite number of sentences, an ability which by no means can be accounted for in terms of finite empirical information that speakers have learnt from the linguistic environment. The second one is the *grammaticality* of speakers, that is, the ability of competent speakers to differentiate between and decide which are the correct or the deviant formulations of language. In order to account for both features, Chomsky constructed an idealization of the knowledge the speaker must possess to be able to speak. Thus, he took as his starting-point an 'ideal speaker–listener, in a completely homogeneous community, who knows his language perfectly and is unaffected by such grammatically irrelevant conditions as memory limitations, distractions, shifts of attention and interest and errors ... in applying his knowledge of the language in actual performance'[45]. This idealization led to the well-known Chomskyan distinction between competence and performance, where performance is the actual speaking of a language in specific circumstances, and competence the underlying structure or the ideal knowledge every speaker must possess in order to account for specific grammatical and creative performances. The competence is, therefore, not restricted to a specific language; it has to be thought in terms of a universal grammar understood as a system of generative rules.

The idea of competence is purely syntactical, however, and does not allow much space for the more semantic and pragmatic dimensions of language. Habermas accepts the Wittgensteinian argument that the rules that make communication possible are intersubjective and pragmatic, and therefore that the grammar of a language game cannot be reduced to the grammatical rules of syntax. In 'Towards a Theory of Communicative Competence', Habermas makes clear that the main problem of Chomsky's theory is his reliance on a Cartesian approach to the subject, where subjects, prior to dialogue, are conceived as *monological* speakers. Chomsky's ideal speaker is also a listener but he is not interacting with other speaker–listeners; he is taken in isolation. Thus, in order to explain the possibility of communication, Chomsky had to assume that all speakers were equipped with the same innate universal system of rules, an assumption that is both too strong and too weak. Indeed, this assumption cannot be empirically demonstrated and it creates an abyss between competence and performance.

Habermas criticized Chomsky's monological approach to competence, but he upheld the Chomskyan idea of a universal grammar that makes language possible. He was himself looking for a deep structure, a generative power or competence[46] that would enable speakers to understand each other. For Habermas, however, this grammar had to account not only for the syntactical, but also for the pragmatic dimension of language. Indeed, the Habermas that criticizes Chomsky had just abandoned the self-reflection framework of his epistemological project and adopted the intersubjective mood of the linguistic turn. He had not, however, given up on his universalist assumptions for critique.

There were other, more radical criticisms of Chomsky, some indeed from within the socio-linguistic community. The term 'communicative competence' used by Habermas had been used by Dell Hymes[47] as an explicit critique of Chomsky's distinction between competence and performance and as a way of questioning the validity of the idea of a *universal* grammar. Chomsky privileged the underlying knowledge the speaker must possess and saw the performance as a secondary moment of application of this knowledge. Hymes argued that the competence should include not just the grammaticality but the *appropriateness* of use. Then competence could no longer be restricted to a syntactical nor even to a semantic system: it had to include the socio-cultural rules of usage. This expansion led inevitably to the collapse of the distinction between competence and performance. The redefinition of competence also changed the theory itself, which could no longer seek the universal features of language as it emphasized the particular features of specific contexts.

As we mentioned, Wittgenstein's approach criticized precisely the view that there is an underlying knowledge, even if we admit that this is a communicative competence, that is, a pragmatic as well as a semantico-syntactical system. Habermas is fully aware of Wittgenstein's anti-general theory stance, a stance derived from his views that language has no deeper essence.[48] The search for a general theory would, for Wittgenstein, be a regression to an understanding of language as knowledge, a view that he continually refused. One of the strategies he used to counterattack this view was to link the grammar of the word 'know' to the grammar of the word 'can', thus showing that to understand something is to do something rather than to 'know' it. In other words, it is the 'mastering of a technique'.[49] More recently, Rorty made this position his own, using not just Wittgenstein's but very similar arguments drawn from the late Heidegger and the American Pragmatists.

Habermas disagrees with Wittgenstein's continual refusal of theory for it completely reduces 'know' to 'can', thereby depriving the argument of its force.[50] In other words, Habermas wants to maintain that language has an objective as well as an interactive dimension, a point which he develops more fully in his later theory of language (universal pragmatics and the theory of communicative action).[51] The retrieval of the theoretical dimension of language, which, according to Habermas, Wittgenstein lost, is central to any theory of communication, including Wittgenstein's own refusal of a general theory.

Moreover, language games are, for Wittgenstein, rule-governed. For Habermas, this rule-governed dimension of language as linguistic practices reveals the necessary agreement between players on what counts as a practice and what counts as a rule. In fact, for Habermas, this agreement is what makes communication possible. Thus, such an agreement could – and should – be the subject matter of a general theory of language, even considering Wittgenstein's point that such an agreement is, of course, a game and, as such, open to new games, that is, to new interpretations.

In fact, Habermas believes that he follows Wittgenstein in the recognition that this agreement is not merely theoretical but pragmatic, or, as Wittgenstein famously put it, that this is an agreement not in opinions, but in forms of life: ' "So you are saying that human agreement decides what is true and what is false?" – It is what human beings say that is true and false, and they agree in the *language* they use. This is not as agreement in opinions but in forms of life.'.[52] Nevertheless, Habermas maintains, this agreement is also the agreement to open communication to critical evaluation. At any time in communication we can question, discuss, and judge the rules and the way we follow what we take to be a rule. This possibility reveals that language is an interactive *and* a cognitive practice. Inbuilt into our capacity for communication is our agreement on the possibility to critically evaluate the rules we use. Habermas argues that, without the recognition of this possibility and the duality of language, we lose the crucial point of language as consisting of language games.[53]

Still, one could point out another dimension of the problem connected to this approach. It could be argued that, in assuming an agreement in language, Habermas might be playing into the hands of a totalitarian and repressive society's wish to silence all forms of dissent. The right to disagree and be different becomes secondary, when we assume the major feature of language to be an agreement or a consensus. We know that strategic action uses force to blow apart any rational attempt to engage in understanding and communication. To think of the Stasi or Pol Pot as derivatives of communication towards understanding is ridiculous. The apparent lack of recognition of this basic fact may seem extraordinary on the part of a seasoned critical theorist such as Habermas. If one looks at Habermas's theory, however, it is clear that the consensus in language he posits is an agreement on the need for emancipation rather than on the need to conform. As we just said, the agreement is an agreement on a practice *and* on the possibility of critically evaluating our performance or the practice itself. Lyotard knows this, though sometimes, for good rhetorical effect, he brandishes the word 'consensus' as a way of fobbing off the appeal of the modernist project. Still, the two have diametrically opposed views on language. It remains to be seen which one provides the better way of developing the idea and practice of justice, for, on the need itself to rethink justice, both authors agree.

Habermas's linguistic turn was always meant to provide the intersubjective norms for critique. The idea of critique is that we can produce a reflection on the distortions and oppressions of power, and that this reflection can promote freedom in our personal, social and natural worlds. As we mentioned before, Habermas's move to language was a way of strengthening this ideal of emancipation, rather than a turning away from it. He feels that if he were to abandon this idea, he could never reclaim, as Lyotard seeks to, a reflection on justice.

The great advantage of language, from a critical theorist's point of view, is that one can show what this mutual agreement can be, as a competence shared by all speakers. Then the gap that plagued the critical theorist's project, namely the distance between the transcendental conditions of possibility and empirical reality, could finally be bridged, by showing that the norms for critique can be found implicitly in everyday ordinary communication. The problem of Habermas's old epistemological project was that it had produced an idea of freedom based on knowledge as science. This knowledge, possessed by a few theorists, not only assumed the questionable view of an avant-garde of critical theorists, but it also separated the idea of freedom from the practice of justice. As Dallmayr pointed out at the time and McCarthy further elaborated,[54] the idea of freedom as self-reflection did not necessarily match an emancipatory practice. The emphasis on language seemed, from the start, to avoid such problems. We all have language, we can all speak. If it could be shown that the mastery of language included more than the linguistic ability to form sentences, if it could be shown that, in speaking something, we also enter into a certain understanding about the validity of what we are saying, Habermas would then have found, in communication, the criteria for judging interactions. By definition, these norms are shared by every competent speaker, that is, by any communicative or interactive human being, in other words, by all of us.

This is precisely what Habermas has done. He has shown, in a compelling way, that successful communication implies three dimensions: the mutual understanding of something; the mutual understanding of the intersubjective relations established in that communication; and the mutual understanding of the validity claims raised by this interaction. These claims form a rational validity basis of speech that can work as norms for our judgement.

In speaking, we produce utterances which must be comprehensible, that is, which must be linguistically well-formed according to linguistic rules. In so doing, we say something about a possible world, that is, we produce an utterance with a propositional content. Moreover, this utterance has also a certain force, according to what we are doing with it, that is, according to the use it has in a certain context. For instance, if I say 'I shall come tomorrow', the affirmation of a propositional content ('I'll come tomorrow') can have the force of a promise or of a threat, according to the circumstances that surround the production of the utterance, which involve the relationships of the partners in communication. In saying something, we are doing more than just saying something; we are engaging in specific relations with ourselves and with others.

This basic insight is, of course, a central tenet of Austin's speech act theory. Austin pointed out that in saying something, we are doing more than describing, accurately or not, a certain state of affairs, true or false. The recognition of this performative dimension of our linguistic acts, so indebted to Wittgenstein, required, according to Austin, a comprehensive and systematic theory of speech acts. This theory had to acknowledge the variety of acts we perform when we speak, and it classified these acts according to what is said, what is done and to what effect, that is, according to the locutionary, illocutionary and perlocutionary forces.[55]

Surprisingly enough, however, this approach can also justify a style of philosophy made famous by the postmodernists. Indeed, it implies that language is no longer a neutral tool for knowledge as accurate description of reality. Truth is no longer a matter of mere description or correspondence to a state of affairs. Austin himself, by no means a relativist, acknowledged in a paper delivered in the future postmodern headquarters – France – that truth is not independent of the context which makes it possible.[56] Saying that 'France is a hexagon' is a perfectly true statement in a first form class, whereas it would probably be meaningless in a Geographical Society meeting, unless it was meant as a reminder of the lack of truth in the knowledge we impart to our children. The recognition that constatives, that is, speech acts concerned with truth, are also performatives, opened up Pandora's box. If truth is to be regulated by the same general conditions of felicity as other speech acts, knowledge and truth no longer possess the special status given to them by traditional philosophy. As noted, not surprisingly by a French author, the idea itself of a *general theory* of speech acts becomes paradoxical, as the idea of such enquiry is undermined by its central finding, namely that speech acts (and there-fore enquiry) are performances rather than statements.[57]

Habermas's reinterpretation of speech act theory tries to escape such paradox and, by the same token, seeks to reassert the project of modernity. Indeed, Habermas wants to demonstrate that, although truth is a language-related concept, it is also an unavoidable ideal for communication. In fact, Habermas wants to show that it is as a language-related concept that truth becomes a grounding ideal for communication. Truth, justice and freedom together form an ideal that makes lan-guage possible, as without it we could never engage in communication. Such an ideal is nothing more than a fiction or an illusion, but it is, as Habermas points out, an '*unavoidable* fiction'[58] or a 'transcendental illusion'.[59]

In order to show this, Habermas moves one step further than speech act theory. He says that, in saying something with a propositional content and an illocutionary force, a speaker is also raising certain validity claims as to the truth of what is said, as to the rightness of the norms that regulate the interaction between speakers and as to the truthfulness of the participants in that communication. Habermas is, of course, not saying that when we speak, we always speak the truth truthfully and rightfully; he is not even saying that we must do so. What he is saying is that when we engage in communication, we mutually expect each other to speak the truth, truthfully and rightfully, and, moreover, we expect reasons to be given in the case where these claims would be thought unfounded. Although we might not share the same ideas of truth, justice and freedom, the fact that we communicate and that we seek to understand each other presupposes that we share the idea that when we speak, we want what is said to be taken as a true, rightful and truthful communica-tion. And, because we do so, we also presume that reasons can be given or sought for the claims we raise. In other words, communication presupposes more than a mutual understanding of something; it also presupposes a mutual understanding of the intersubjective validity of what has been understood as claims that can be ratio-nally redeemed.

We can see here how distant Habermas is from the idea that there is a factual consensus grounding our understanding of meaning. In speaking, speakers raise validity claims and they agree not so much on their content as on the possibility of redeeming these claims through rational argumentation. Of course, there is no guarantee that an agreement will ever be reached, nor that, if ever reached, such an agreement could not be further discussed and possibly changed. Habermas seeks to reclaim the notions of truth, rightness (justice) and truthfulness (authenticity, freedom) as the universal conditions of possibility of language, but these condi-tions are not necessarily met or realized. Habermas's universalism, so to speak, allows for the particular differences that are the everyday reality of our multicultural societies. But it also stresses what binds us together as speaking subjects (albeit of different languages). This binding is the rationality of communication as an interaction which makes validity claims that can always be discussed at the level of discourse.

For Habermas, discourse is the level of argumentation that can lead to a 'good consensus', that is, a rationally motivated one, freed from distortions of power. The conditions under which such consensus is possible stress the need for a symmetrical situation in all uses of speech, not only cognitive, but also interactive and expressive. The point here goes beyond the postmodernist relativism regarding truth. Indeed, Habermas's theory of discourse shows how critical reflection on a truth claim might call into question the frame of reference that makes a certain agreement on truth possible, thus recognizing that these frames are contingent and practically motivated. Habermas's point goes even further. For him, a good consensus involves more than the cognitive dimension in that it also involves the other uses of speech. Thus, the symmetry of critical argumentation – the basis for a rationally motivated consensus – has to be matched by the symmetry of equal roles and opportunities to speak for all possible partners, and by the search by all participants for a deeper understanding or even a transparency of their inner nature.[60] What this means is that the validity basis of speech does not involve a return to epistemology. The validity basis of speech shows that communication presupposes a background of mutual recognition of autonomous and responsible subjectivities, claiming to speak the truth, truthfully and rightfully. This is not so much a cognitive deed as an *ethical imperative*. The possibility of understanding relies on this structure, which is really the mutual recognition of autonomy and freedom as ideas and claims we mutually expect and impute to each other. Without these we would not be able to communicate.

In Habermas's theory of communicative action, the competence of the speakers is not reducible to knowledge; it is the mutual recognition of the participants' claims to be seen as autonomous subjects capable of speaking the truth, possessing judgement and aspiring to a just society. The level of discourse recognizes that the 'good reasons' that can be invoked for the redemption of the validity claims do not constitute a purely cognitive argument. They are the ethical recognition that an ideal of a just and free society is built into a situation of communicative understanding. Undoubtedly, our violent multicultural societies are not the best examples of understanding, dedicated, as sometimes they are, to 'ethnic cleansing' and to the hatred of differences. These are cases where communication has broken down. Nevertheless, the everyday fact of ordinary communication shows our continuous presumption of and attempts to produce a better understanding. And Habermas shows how this understanding implies an agreement on the validity basis of language, an agreement that presupposes that we mutually recognize each other as speakers ideally capable of discussing and giving good reasons for judging our actions, on the basis of our (intersubjectively constituted) ideas of truth, justice and freedom.

Lyotard suspects Habermas of clinging to a cognitivist strategy, as for him such an agreement does not exist; moreover, he is also suspicious of the 'good reasons' invoked. For him, these good reasons are too close to the scientific validation of truth. For Habermas, however, this agreement, to paraphrase Wittgenstein, is not an agreement on knowledge; it is an agreement on a form of life. Lyotard's questioning of Habermas's approach to language as consensus does not do justice to the change of perspective produced by his linguistic turn. In fact, Habermas is pointing to the possibility of subverting a consensus by relying on nothing more than language itself and the ideals it incorporates. Here we could think of the cases of regimes which, in their attempt to deny the autonomy of their citizens, have used as a weapon the flattening and banalization of communication. The 'power of the powerless' as V. Havel showed in his famous paper,[61] consisted of the use of the emancipatory potential built into language, even in the most fossilized use of Marxist slogans. Because we can speak, we can always turn language around and reveal the truth of our necessary ideal of autonomy. This example supports Habermas's view that all communication is derivative from understanding. What he is claiming is that even the least truthful, right or true interaction still assumes, by the very fact that we are communicating, that such an agreement, or at least a discussion on these values, can be produced in language. On this 'unavoidable fiction' rests, says Habermas, the 'humanity of mankind'.[62] This is a possible strategy in language, however, not a reality that can be demonstrated in every act of speech.

Lyotard's suspicions of a strong cognitivist bent in Habermas's programme are not totally unfounded. Sometimes Habermas seems to forget that this ideal in language is an illusion and treats it as an empirical reality, to be uncovered by science. In 'What is Universal Pragmatics', Habermas proposed a reconstructive science, which attempted to show how every speech act had a deeper structure, revealing the validity basis of speech.[63] This reconstruction was based on Searle's problematic principle of expressibility, which claims that every speech act can be adequately expressed by an explicit speech act in the standard form of the expression $F(p)$ where F is the force and (p) the propositional content.[64] This is, however, not necessarily the case. To shout 'Fire!' is not the same as to say 'I warn you that the house is on fire'.[65] As Thompson argued, without the principle of expressibility, the idea that every speech act (and not just speech acts of the standard form) raises all three validity claims becomes questionable.[66]

In fact, Habermas's attempt to show that an analysis of speech acts reveals the deeper structure of speech endangers the idea of the validity basis of speech. To show that the mutual recognition of intersubjectivity as autonomy is, as a transcendental *fiction*, a condition of understanding is to stress the recourse we, as competent speakers, can have to an ideal of autonomy and freedom, not yet realized, for the maintenance of understanding. To show – or to attempt to show – that such an ideal grounds *every* single act of speech is to misunderstand its transcendental dimension and to treat it as an empirical reality. Then the intersubjectivity of language as the mutual recognition of our constituting and constitutive idealizations can become the attribute of a subjectivity that actually grounds language. The recognition of the 'other' of language as that which is not and can never be fully known, which Lyotard correctly emphasizes in his approach, can be forgotten. Reason, once again, can come dangerously close to an ideal of positivistic knowledge, thus endangering the very move towards discourse and ethics which Habermas proposed.

The move towards language was based on the recognition by Habermas that rationality and knowledge needed to take into account the relations with others and with ourselves that formed our processes of thinking. Thus, freedom and justice were not a product of science but a precondition, as an ideal, of the very possibility of creating true knowledge. In other words, ethics could not be viewed as an afterthought of the scientific mind nor as a branch of scientific (or critical theory) enquiry. The possibility of an intersubjective world of autonomous and responsible subjects is an indispensable part of our ideal of truth as a language-related concept. Habermas's strategy, however, relied too heavily on demonstrating the anticipation in *every* speech act, on an ideal of communication as truth, justice and freedom. This demonstration made the status of this ideal ('transcendental illusion') too close to an empirical reality. The idea of a reconstructive science also placed a misleading emphasis on theoretical knowledge, thus paving the way for a misinterpretation of what Habermas considers good reasons in discourse.

Lyotard disagrees with the view that there is a fundamental agreement between all speaking subjects, even in the sense that their competence as speakers involves the recognition of mutual expectations as a rational validity basis of speech. For him, language is a battleground where irreconcilable differences constantly fight each other. For Habermas, there must be an agreement even for a disagreement to be possible. Language is understanding. In spite of his acknowledgement of the incommensurability of language games, Habermas also stresses the understanding that must underlie the recognition of these differences. The facts that these differences exist and that a total transparency is never achieved, do not undermine the basic assumption that in so far as we speak, we aim at understanding, therefore we aim at communication, albeit from different horizons or perspectives. There is some form of understanding that makes the idea of distance and misunderstanding possible, even as a working concept. In this sense, Habermas's emphasis on understanding, that is, on what makes communication possible, serves as a reminder of the strategies opened up by language. The problem of Habermas's theory of communicative action does not lie in his emphasis on understanding; rather it lies in *what he denies* in order to make his case stronger. Then the illusion of the ideal speech situation becomes the reality of speech acts, the 'unknown' of reason becomes known and his whole conception of truth, justice and freedom as language-related notions is endangered.

Because of this emphasis, Habermas is no longer interested in psychoanalysis or in psychoanalytical understanding of knowledge and rationality. Previously, his interest in Freud (and Marx) followed from his interest in a type of knowledge where the subjects were vaguely aware of what they did not know, that is, a knowledge that acknowledged that it was shaped by reasons unknown. Still, the difficulties of this approach for a defence of modernity made him ask these questions in a rather different manner.

In one of the early papers on the linguistic turn, 'On Systematically Distorted Communication' (Habermas, 1970a), Habermas asked how he should address pseudo-communications. In these cases, participants do not recognize any disturbance in communication, but, due to this non-recognition and to a false consensus, they produce continuous and reciprocal misunderstandings. This paper treated psychoanalysis as a type of communication that helped overcome these distortions. It also stressed how psychoanalytical theory had to have an ideal of a normal communication, in order to decode meanings that had become privatized. From there to 'What is Universal Pragmatics', where Habermas wishes to reconstruct scientifically the validity basis of speech, there is a continuity. This continuity emphasizes the knowledge that we must have, that is, the agreement that is available in language. Still, there is also a loss, as Habermas seems less concerned with what is *not* known though it might distort what is known. Reconstructive sciences are aimed precisely at reconstructing, from the display of competences, the universal structures of speech and action. For this task, Piaget and Kohlberg, who produced theories of the cognitive and moral stages of development, are better allies than psychoanalytical thinking. Once again, the problem here is not the historical and cultural contingencies of such structures, which Habermas recognizes and which the neo-Piagetians and Kohlbergian approaches allow for. The problem is that in order to maintain their universality, Habermas abstracts these competences, as Piaget and Kohlberg do, from the world of actually lived experience. Reason, however, is not just conscious, argumentative knowledge, but also includes the dimension of the unconscious, which shapes our experiences of the world and our reasons for living the way we do.

There is a fundamental misconception in thinking about the process of thinking as an abstract cognitive process. Of course, this assumption – reason as an abstract process – was closely associated with the epistemological framework and the myth of an isolated subjectivity. With his linguistic turn, Habermas took the view that all discursive thinking takes place in language and that language is an intersubjective structure. Thus, I do not think alone, but with categories and with other subjects, in a fundamentally dialogical process. Habermas still privileges, however, a certain type of abstract thinking – argumentative reasoning – and this creates a distance between reason and our experience of the world. In fact, thinking is making links, a process that starts even pre-verbally as concrete perceptions of our relations to others.

In psychoanalysis, there was a similar move from knowledge to language. The move was from an economic theory of drives and sexuality, which in a sense still privileged the idea of an isolated subjectivity with libidinal discharges, to an emphasis on the *objects* (the other persons) of these drives,[67] a shift that privileged the *relational* aspect of the emotional and instinctual life. For Freud, and we shall come back to this discussion in Chapter 4, when we discuss Freud and Klein, pleasure and reality can be said to be economic principles, in the sense that the pleasure principle is related to the increase or reduction in quantities of excitation, with the reality principle modifying the search for pleasure according to the state of the outside world.[68] For Klein, these principles are seen in terms of the interaction that takes place between subjects (objects or part-objects) from the very start of life. In a sense, Klein fully integrated in psychoanalysis the phenomenological insight into the intentionality of consciousness, an insight that came originally from psychology, from Brentano. The Kleinian school of thought approaches the infant as a *relating* person from the very early beginning, thus creating the 'object-relations theory', a misleading term, as 'object' means the other person (or certain aspects or parts of that person) to whom one is relating.

Needless to say, Klein does not attribute to the infant the mature capacities of adulthood. It was precisely her interest in very early emotional stages, however, that enabled her to show these primitive forms of *relating*. Some Kleinian-inspired research[69] has even examined, with the help of intra-uterine ultrasound techniques, the ways a foetus relates to the womb or, in the case of twins, to the other, with some very interesting follow-ups later on in childhood. The infant relates to the object or 'part'-objects, a term that acknowledges that relationships do not in general presume a mutual recognition of the other as an autonomous, fully-integrated individual. This is a much later achievement, influenced, and sometimes hampered, by the early forms of relating. For Klein, the infant feeding at the breast cannot be reduced to the satisfaction and release of instinctual energy. It is the establishment of a relationship that involves an extremely rich world of fantasies in terms of how the infant perceives the breast (as a good or as a bad object) and how it relates to it (by attacking it or by loving its care). For Klein and Bion, the capacity for thinking is related to these very early, pre-verbal and yet intersubjective and therefore communicative experiences of the world.

The most interesting feature of this move, which is similar to the philosophical move from the monological to the dialogical subject, is that object-relations theory is a theory of *thinking*. Many purists accused Melanie Klein of abandoning Freud's theory of sexuality. This is not the case, though the emphasis did shift from a theory of sexual development to what we do to our objects in different phases of development. The focus of this approach was the way we establish, from the very outset of life, relations to others or parts of others, and how these relations constitute links lying at the core of our capacity for thinking. If we approach mental life in this way, then inevitably the emphasis shifts from a purely cognitive, abstract mental development, as, say, in Piaget, to a recognition of the fundamental role of our interrelations with others.[70] This is not merely a recognition of the 'emotional' aspect of our intellectual life, for this would imply a privileging of the emotional over the cognitive. What this approach shows is how thinking processes are inextricably interwoven with concrete emotional experiences in relation to ourselves and, most importantly, in relation to others. The baby that cries discharges an unpleasurable excitation in the mother, but, in so doing, it also communicates something to her, a communication that, if taken up by the mother in a process that Bion called 'reverie' and Winnicott 'containment', can be digested and given back to the infant.[71] In the process, the infant also introjects an object that can 'digest' and make links. The reintegration of what was felt to be unbearable, now contained, allows for further links to be made and for thoughts to be formed.[72] When, for various reasons, such development is hindered, it is generally the capacity for thinking and for symbol formation which is affected, together with emotional problems. The unpleasurable excitation is then felt to be part of the bad breast and identified with it. The 'attack' on the breast, that is, the baby's own unpleasurable excitation, is now projected onto the breast, which becomes a 'bad breast'. This, however, can only lead to more anxiety, as the bad breast is now feared as a source of possible retaliatory and persecutory damage rather than as a source of pleasure.

One might understandably reply that a pre-verbal infant would be incapable of such 'mind-games'. The interest of reading Kleinian literature lies in its extensive clinical research, particularly with babies and children. In reading Kleinian literature, one's eyes are open to the ways children – and adults – function, and the above description is not too far off the mark. When a child bumps against a door, she or he becomes furious at the door. When a small child does something wrong (say, breaking the arm of a favourite doll or making a tower of bricks collapse), if he is upset enough, he will scream at his mother, 'You made me do it!' or 'You did it!', followed by 'I hate you!' He might then run away in fear of the retaliation by the mother who might indeed (or in his fantasy) respond to this projection of the child's unwanted, clumsy parts. As adults, we are not immune either to this 'childish' behaviour, as our small daily irritations (against husbands and wives, bus and train conductors, for instance) reveal, and as a closer look at our insane rages against other races or nationalities more seriously exposes.

The work of Kleinians with children and psychotics has shown how previously meaningless forms of communication could be understood following this approach. Thus, bizarre forms of language or actions, as well as the apparent absence of communication in autistic children, can be understood as a lack of freedom of imagination, as a breakdown in the capacity for symbolization.[73] Thought and symbols are then used in a distorted form, where instead of allowing for the imaginative creation, play and communication of language, they remain attached to a very concrete, bizarre meaning. In a well-known paper, 'Notes on Symbol Formation', H. Segal argues that symbols can become very concrete objects, which she calls a 'symbolic equation'. These unconscious symbols, or 'bizarre' objects as Bion called them, were epitomized by Segal's schizophrenic patient who could no longer play the violin in front of an audience as he could not possibly masturbate in public! She contrasted this case with that of a patient who *dreamt* of playing the violin with his girlfriend but who was able to recognize the masturbatory fantasies associated with his dream. In the schizophrenic case, one witnesses a concreteness of thinking that reduces and freezes his world, as he can no longer distinguish between his fantasies, his projections and his splittings, and the real world of intersubjective actions. The boundaries between the baby and the breast, between I and Thou, between my attack and the retaliatory persecutions I imagine, are blurred. We just attempt to survive the fear that these bad objects create by further splittings that will, in their turn, come back to haunt us.

It is also interesting to note that, in terms of technique, Kleinians are more interested in what the patients *do* rather than in what they *say* in the psychoanalytical session. Needless to say, this is not a concern with their physical actions as opposed to their verbal actions. Indeed, the emphasis here is on the recognition that the content of the material brought can be used for various purposes in the course of a session. It is fundamental not to take the actions, verbal or otherwise, of the patient as a monologue but as a communication, in the transference setting, of an emotional experience.

Something similar can be seen in our ways of thinking about ourselves as members of a culture or of a social group. When our world is sharply divided between the good and the bad, 'us' the good and 'they' the bad, and when these distinctions have to be maintained at all costs, for otherwise the precarious balance of our identity might collapse, then we are generally using any means to maintain such fictions, even if the price of this 'defence' is to obliterate and exterminate 'them' and our thinking capacity in the process. What psychoanalysis has shown is that the price paid is not just that of being on the morally condemnable side of the exterminators, though this is indeed the case. This, in a sense, is not enough, as the Nazis probably saw themselves as the 'cleansers' rather than the 'soilers'. The price to be paid is that we attack our own capacity for thinking and making links. In this respect, it is highly illuminating to read Hannah Arendt's account of Eichmann's trial in Jerusalem[74] and how his lack of humanity struck her as a lack of capacity for thought. The report, as we know, provoked an enormous controversy, as it was seen by some as a justification for Eichmann's actions. Arendt's point was more profound, and in no sense did it exculpate Eichmann. Her point was that evil destroys thinking and understanding, and that without this understanding, we are left with no humanity. Precisely because this understanding is what makes us human, we are and must be accountable at the highest level for its destruction and the horror that inevitably follows.

Habermas, as we know, agrees with the recognition that what makes us human is our capacity for thought and reason, which has to be understood as a striving for justice, truth and freedom. But unless we recognize that thinking and reason, as measures of our humanity, are not abstract developmental processes, but concrete emotional experiences developed from very early interactions, we may not fully comprehend the level of unconscious fantasies that shape our more mature abstract reasoning and argumentative processes. For Habermas, the Enlightenment ideal of rational autonomy and happiness is pursued through his respect for the separateness and difference of the other subject as an equal partner in discourse. But unless we start to comprehend and accept the mechanisms that can destroy the recognition of the other, we might not do justice to the very ideal we are striving for. The fundamental contribution of psychoanalysis to such a project is the recognition that our capacity for thinking and tolerating separateness and difference has to acknowledge an unconscious world which can attack the most basic links that make understanding possible. It also shows that the unconscious, unknown world encompasses more than can be known by 'abstract', purely cognitive processes.

3

LYOTARD'S LINGUISTIC TURN

The strength of Lyotard's project is the way in which he unwaveringly chooses to say what cannot be said. He thrives on the difficulties engendered by such a paradox. He feels closer to the laughter of the sophist, to the pleasure that playing with reason, turning order around and pushing logic to its limits, can give. Lyotard deliberately chooses to abandon reason as a purveyor of knowledge and thus, turns his back on what we called the epistemological project.

Lyotard's critique of knowledge has highlighted the transformation that knowledge has undergone, and the inadequacy of a modernist critique. In *The Postmodern Condition*, he showed how knowledge in contemporary societies has become technically efficient knowledge, translatable into marketable and computerized information. The characteristically modern questions, typical of the Enlightenment, as, for instance, the questions of the truth, justice and morality of knowledge, have become reduced to questions of efficiency, marketing and profit. The idea of knowledge as a 'savoir-faire' or a 'savoir-vivre', that is, knowledge as an activity that encompasses more of life, has all but disappeared in the information technology world of today. This, as we know, is a critique of knowledge and technology with which Habermas, who wrote 'Science and Technology as Ideology' (Habermas, 1980), would undoubtedly agree. The main disagreement, however, is that Lyotard believes that philosophy, and not just science and technology, has also contributed to this impoverishment of knowledge. Philosophy has traditionally believed in science as a model for knowledge, sometimes overlooking the circumstances that surround the production of any type of knowledge. Thus, for Lyotard, philosophy has promoted the myth of science as the only purveyor of truth, the ultimate story about all other possible stories, in any time or space. Philosophy itself, mainly as epistemology, has become a universal 'Grand Narrative', that is, a story that purports to tell the truth and reveal the meaning of all other stories. Thus, language is reduced to denotation, a tool for knowledge with no senders and no addressees. In this way, language simply reports a reality which exists outside itself, a severe limitation, notwithstanding how important or vital this report might be.

Lyotard's linguistic turn follows Wittgenstein's approach to language as consisting of language games. This approach refuses the very idea of a definition or an essence of language, as it highlights the diversity and heterogeneity of possible language games. Language games involve concrete speakers engaging in various forms of activities and relationships, activities which are not merely reports and knowledge, but constitute possible forms of life. Lyotard's specific contribution is his stress on the heterogeneity and incommensurability, not just of language games, but of the activities, the speakers and the phrases within them. There is no unity and no essence of language. Language for him is 'agonistic', that is, a space of disputes and conflict (from the Greek 'agon') which can never be settled. The differences are incommensurable. There is no other game, no other language and no other phrase that could reconcile these differences. The idea of justice for Lyotard, as we shall see later, stems from the realization that these differences cannot and *should not* be settled, as they are fundamentally irreconcilable. Any settlement or any attempt to reconcile these heterogeneous voices must necessarily repress and exclude that which cannot be couched in the language of the settlement (Lyotard calls it the '*différend*'). The dream of a last judgement, of a language without conflict and difference is, for Lyotard, the idea of violence to and oppression of the '*différend*'. Lyotard explicitly wishes to adopt a style of writing which avoids the reduction of philosophy to theory, by evoking and showing the disputes, the conflicts and the diversity that form the heterogeneity that we call language.[75]

Lyotard is aware, however, that such a critique is part of knowledge itself, in so far as it forms a theoretical and therefore an epistemological position. Indeed, if Lyotard argues against theories, saying that there are no universal judgements, if he says that a perspective is always bound by its circumstances, his position is, of course, open to the same criticism. When he says that there are no universal statements, just particular instances, he is producing a universal statement which then becomes relative to the circumstances of its production and therefore loses its power.

Lyotard is not afraid of these paradoxes. Indeed, he wants to dwell on them as part of his project of saying what cannot be said. He wants to show the side of reason where reason – or at least logic and cognitive rules – does not apply. His move to language, unlike that of Habermas, is meant not simply as an overcoming of epistemology, but as a conscious option for the 'other' of reason, for that which cannot be thought. He clearly delights in the paradoxes of reason, paradoxes the alleged solutions to which have been incorporated in the history of philosophy, as triumphs of rational knowledge. What Lyotard shows is how short-lived these triumphs are. From his point of view, it is the sophist who has the last laugh, by making the paradox his trade. And, like him, Lyotard chooses language as an alternative to knowledge, rhetoric rather than theory. It could be said that this choice is guided by Hermes, the god of language, the messenger of the gods who inspired the creation of hermeneutics. But if this could be called a 'hermeneutic' move, it is not a scientific one; it is Hermes the trickster, not the patron of a science, who attracts Lyotard to the pleasures of creating confusion and laughter amongst gods and humans.

For someone who says, 'There are no universal judgements', the paradox involved in the assertion of 'I always lie' is a particularly delightful one. Lyotard shows that the traditional philosophical solution to it is no solution. Indeed, in order to make the problem disappear, the philosopher isolates what is being said from what was said, the present from the past. Thus, if I say, 'I have always lied' rather than, 'I always lie', the paradox disappears, even if I do not make my distancing move explicit. By privileging the moment of reflection as if it were an atemporal moment, the philosopher thinks he avoids these paradoxes. Lyotard's argument against the traditional narrative of philosophy is that it treats the present as if it were a moment outside time, as if I could look back on the past or forward to the future without my present self and my present reflection being part of the temporal flux. Descartes is the obvious culprit who comes to mind. Indeed, in *Meditations* he famously imagined time as composed of isolated parts which were not interdependent, thus protecting his reflection from the doubts and uncertainties he was exploring.[76] This approach to time is, of course, the setting-stone for the myth of an atemporal and self-contained subjectivity. Moreover, by attempting to depict knowledge as located in an atemporal moment of reflection, independent of the cultural and historical circumstances that produce it, the philosopher creates the fiction of Western narratives as a superior form of knowledge. Such an atemporal form of knowledge must be superior to other narratives, which are bound by temporal and spatial circumstances. This fiction creates the grounds for knowledge as oppression, exclusion and domination.

The liar paradox arises from the affirmation of a propositional content ('I am a liar') which contradicts the sincerity of the affirmation. The affirmation and its simultaneous contradiction, however, can only come about as a speech act, that is, as an act that happens in time and in a certain context. It is only as an act brought about by a speaker in the temporal flux that an affirmation can refer to and contradict itself. To take away this reflexivity by isolating the propositional content from the speech act in its wider, spatial and temporal context might apparently solve the paradox. But, in so doing, one is depriving language of precisely the ordinariness which is also its richness. Logicians have dreamt of creating a 'better' artificial language that would avoid these paradoxes, but, in so doing, they have created second-order languages that cannot do what ordinary language does, leading to an infinite regression, as this second order requires another and then another level for reflection.

Wittgenstein's critique of Russell's logical atomism in *Philosophical Investigations* follows these lines. Russell, of course, made the self-reference paradox famous ('All Cretans are liars.'). In a sense, a similar problem arises in his theory of types, where a proposition that refers to a set of propositions cannot itself belong to that set. To solve it, Russell created classes that do not contain themselves, but this solution had to be endlessly repeated, with the problem reappearing at each new creation of classes. Again, the search for an artificial language or the move to another order of language seems to solve the problem at first, when, in fact, the moment this artificial language is created, the moment it is spoken or thought, the problem inevitably reappears. I cannot isolate the present from time, or, if I choose

39

this strategy, I do it as part of language, in time. There is no outside point from which I can look at all reality at once.

The sophist's dispute between Protagoras, the teacher, and his student, Euathlus, reveals the impossibility of solving such riddles. Protagoras, the best-known sophist and the author of the famous relativist motto 'Man is the measure of all things', demanded payment from his student Euathlus, who refused on the grounds that he, Euathlus, had never won a litigation. Their agreement was that Protagoras would teach Euathlus to argue so that the student would win at least one dispute. They decided to settle their difference in a litigation, and, said Protagoras, if he, Protagoras, won, Euathlus should pay, for he, Protagoras, would have won. But if Euathlus won, he should still pay Protagoras for Euathlus would have won and therefore Protagoras would have won once again, as he would have fulfilled his part of their deal. For Lyotard, the impossibility of settling Protagoras' and Euathlus' dispute[77] is another example of how language speaks as it is spoken, in time. There cannot be a last judgement or an atemporal language. All judgements are judged, language is never final and there is always another sentence that can be added, another set for Russell's theory. The logician's recourse has been exposed by showing the infinity or, more accurately, the temporality of language.

In the 1980s, Derek Freeman starred in and produced a film intended 'to set the record straight' on Margaret Mead's well-known ethnographic study of Samoa.[78] Mead's study was explicitly intended as a tool for rethinking American attitudes towards what was then thought of as a purely biological development, namely adolescent sexuality. By showing the comparatively freer and less demanding mores of Samoan adolescents, Mead hoped to change American educational attitudes.[79] To counteract what he saw as a cornerstone of relativism, Freeman proposed to bring forward the ultimate truth: the physical presence of one of Mead's informants from 1925, who affirms on camera that she and her friends just 'lied and lied'. Her physical presence and the supposed neutrality of the camera-eye only enhances our postmodern pleasure at hearing the 'truth' from a self-acknowledged liar. This debate was particularly interesting for it also drew one's attention to the dangers of a radical critique of relativism. Indeed, for Freeman, it seemed as if the only resort left against relativism (the precursor of our contemporary postmodernism) is to claim that there are certain features of physical reality or nature which escape the variety of cultural differences, the very differences that the anthropologist is supposed to be concerned with. He had hoped to settle the dispute by bringing in the ultimate evidence, the informant herself. This, of course, is a denial of the constitutional role of meaning and language for any 'natural' reality, a denial that culminates in the paradox of his witness as a self-acknowledged liar.

It is not just the *tour de force* of rhetoric and sophistry that appeals to Lyotard. It is the challenge of showing that we are fascinated by, and take a particular pleasure in, a type of thinking that defies thinking, a type of logic that laughs at logic. In fact, the particular grip that this type of 'antilogic' exerts is similar to the pleasure we take in certain works of art, or in the not-so-absurd absurdity of our dreams.

Indeed, this type of 'antilogic' brings us closer to the 'logic' of the unconscious, as Freud described it.[80]

For Freud, the unconscious was a system which was radically different from consciousness and even from the wider ensemble of ideas that are yet not conscious but that can become so at some point. In other words, for Freud, the term 'the unconscious' was not a purely descriptive qualification, as that which is outside consciousness. For him, the unconscious (Ucs) is a different system from consciousness (Cs and Pcs) where different rules apply. Indeed, the logic of the unconscious, ruled by the pleasure principle, is the logic of 'wishful impulses'. These instinctual impulses exist side by side; they do not contradict and they do not exclude each other. They can even become the 'other' as they do in dreams or in jokes. If there is a conflict, say, between two impulses, they might form an intermediary aim, but they will not deny each other. As Freud remarked, in the unconscious there is 'no doubt, no degrees of certainty'.[81] The logic of the unconscious works through processes of displacement and condensation, rather than according to the laws of contradiction and negation, made possible by repression. The clarity of logic, with the principle of non-contradiction, is linked to the repression of unconscious fantasies, a repression that is part of the preconscious system which forbids the access to consciousness of unconscious thoughts and emotions.

We recognize in the sophist's laughter the particular pleasure of showing that logic becomes antilogic at the extreme limits of rationality. Thinking can be turned inside out or upside down, and the security of a world of identities and non-contradiction fragments. By playing with language, the sophist talks about that which cannot be said. Indeed, the moment it is spoken, it must undergo the censorship of the Cs-Pcs system and therefore change. Freud remarks on this laughter as a sign of the mixture of elements belonging to the unconscious and the preconscious.[82] Lyotard's interest in language and art reveals his pleasure in the unconscious and his delight in showing that what is thought contains that which escapes the logic of reason. Indeed, his conception of postmodernity is at its best when conceived as the idea of presenting the unpresentable.

Lyotard's definition of postmodernity, paradoxically enough, is closest to Kant's definition of the sublime. Kant, the champion of modernity, defines the sublime as the distance between, on one hand, our capacity for conceiving the sublime and, on the other hand, the impossibility of actually presenting an object in accordance with such concepts. We have the ideas of the world, of the simple, of the absolutely big or the absolutely powerful, but we do not have the capacity for exhibiting an example of these ideas. Such ideas have no possible presentation; they are unpresentable and therefore not related to our faculty of understanding (cognition). The idea of presenting the unpresentable, Kant's idea of the sublime, is Lyotard's idea of what is at stake in art and language, as the epitome of postmodernity.[83]

This impossibility of presenting the unpresentable can take two modes. One, which Lyotard terms 'nostalgic', deplores the limits of our faculty of presentation and tries to enlarge this capacity for knowledge. The other mode, which Lyotard calls 'novatio', excels in the power of inventing new modes and new rules. This mode can only lead to the *widening* of the gap between what is presentable and what is conceivable.[84] At many points in his writings, Lyotard lets us believe that modernity dwells exclusively on the nostalgic mode, as it concentrates on developing our capacity for presentation. The strong criticisms, in *The Post Modern Condition*, of science and the role it plays in the 'Grand Narrative' of modernity, are indications of this identification of knowledge with modernity. Here, postmodernity would be the creation of new modes, the surpassing of presentation, of modernity's enchantment with knowledge.[85]

The only problem with this type of reading is that it forgets that what makes the sublime, in Lyotard's own reading of Kant, is the *tension* between what is knowable and what is conceivable. For Kant, the critical reflection on the faculties of reason leads to the recognition that there are, in pure reason, antinomies that cannot be solved by understanding alone. For Kant, these antinomies reflect the duality of our relation to knowledge of the world, as noumena and phenomena. This duality is the recognition of the impossibility of absolute knowledge. This recognition is eminently rational, however, and by no means leads to a disenchantment with reason. For Kant, the limitations of pure reason call for a moral critique of and a practical engagement with the world. These tasks, however, are rational. If Lyotard were indeed claiming that modernity reduces reason to understanding, and that postmodernity opens the space of playfulness and inventiveness, then postmodernity could no longer think the sublime as the *tension* between conceiving and presenting. The questions of judgement and our practical engagement in the world would no longer be rational problems when, for Kant, they are the central questions of the critiques.

This is also a central idea in Freud's understanding of mental life as that which is both conscious and unconscious. Freud, in fact, refers to Kant in his justification of the concept of the unconscious, so fundamental to psychoanalytical theory.[86] He acknowledges his indebtedness to Kant in his view that the objects themselves, be they in the external (physical) or in the internal (mental) world, are not the same as the objects presented to consciousness. The question here is not so much the correctness of Freud's reading of Kant's understanding of the duality of knowledge. Freud is a true heir to the Enlightenment because, unlike Lyotard, his recognition of the limits of rationality *creates* the possibility of a knowledge of mental life that allows for the unconscious, that is, for that which can only be known once it ceases to be unconscious. Indeed, Freud, in spite of the pessimism that came to haunt the end of his life, believed that, whilst we can never know the unconscious as such, its presentation to consciousness offers an access to and even a possibility of a transformation of this unconscious world. The joke, the dream, the slips of the tongue all speak, though they use a language that allows the forbidden to be said. The teacher who unintentionally calls himself a 'cheat' in front of a class can laugh with his students at his 'joke' (or at his own anxiety). The dream as a wish fulfilment of a censored instinctual impulse is a compromise formation, but one that nevertheless allows for a certain access to the unconscious mental reality.

The nostalgic mode of modernity does not necessarily mean, as Lyotard sometimes implies, a nostalgia for the dream of a presentation of the whole object (or a
thorough 'chimney sweeping' of the unconscious, as many patients of analysis
expect). The recognition of the inevitable distance between conceiving and presenting is a recognition produced in consciousness, through knowledge and our
faculty of understanding. Still, the idea of what knowledge, rationality and understanding are must change. For Kant, the project of modernity is a defence of rationality that recognizes the bounds of reason. For Freud also, psychoanalysis is an
eminently rational theory and practice, which aims at transforming and understanding that which is unconscious and therefore radically different from what is
consciously known.

Lyotard, however, sometimes believes that to speak of the unconscious 'in the
name of reason' and knowledge as Kant and Freud do, is to betray the fundamental
insight into the 'other' of reason as radically 'other'. For him, to create a science of
mental life which acknowledges the unconscious is to deny the unconscious and
promote the moment of repression as 'rational thought'. This identification of
Western rationality with exclusion and totalitarianism is the main shortcoming of
Lyotard's project,[87] a shortcoming that seriously endangers his own wish for justice. The recognition that knowledge is not a purely abstract process, but a lived
experience of emotional and unconscious fantasies which shapes what we call our
understanding of ourselves and others, should not mean the end of knowledge;
rather, it could be the beginning of a less omnipotent but more real acceptance of
the contradictions and mysteries of our own lives. Knowledge is not *per se* a violence. Nevertheless, to conceive knowledge as an abstract understanding distinct
from the more encompassing life of unconscious fantasies might indeed promote a
violence towards understanding. Still, we do want to know and, as Habermas so
compellingly points out, the search for communication implies a wish to reach an
implicit understanding about what we are saying as making claims to be intelligible, true, just and free from distortions of power.

The idea of a universal truth is very easily proved 'wrong' by the sophist. But
then so is the relativist assumption as an assumption, as Lyotard himself shows.[88]
What this debate illustrates (as does the laughter of the sophist) is that these universal claims cannot be 'proved'. As we saw with the case of Derek Freeman's film,
the choice cannot be limited to one between relativist lies and universal 'truths' to
be found in 'nature' (the physical presence of the informant who says she lied and
lied). The alternative to relativism should not be positivism; the alternative to the
postmodern laughter is a modernity that recognizes the problems of reflexivity and
can look at its own limitations.[89] This recognition does not mean, however, the
abandonment of the idea of a universal, displayed in our striving for understanding
in communication. To give up this idea is to give up the search for a type of life that
acknowledges the greatest possible number of different perspectives, or, in other
words, a type of knowledge that fosters and protects difference and debate. The
fact that we recognize that universals can never be established independently of
situated discussions and debates does not mean that we have to give up the wish for

a life where justice, truth and freedom would be universal. This wish is implied in the goals of communication and it guides our ideas of democracy and freedom which are, of course, situated, historical forms of life. Without these universalistic principles, we cannot articulate a critique of our temporal, situated ideals of democracy.[90] What Habermas has given us is an understanding of reason as both the universal and the particular, that is, reason as involving claims to universal principles that can (and should) be discursively redeemed in particular, not universal, situations. Without this striving for the universal, the idea of reason and judgement disappears as one possible story amongst so many other stories. The defence of differences and heterogeneity can only be maintained within the universalist framework of the ideas of justice and freedom for all.

Lyotard's contribution to this project is his capacity for understanding how, unknown to us and unwittingly, knowledge can come to constitute a violence to justice. Indeed, Lyotard shows how and why we sometimes promote, *in the name of reason*, the violence that knowledge was supposed to overcome. Habermas's approach to knowledge does not allow for this particular twist. Lyotard creates new ways of talking and thinking about that which silences thought and reason. He promotes an understanding of language and reason as a place of conflict, oppression and repression. In other words, he allows for the unconscious world of wishes and fantasies which might go *against* language as communication towards understanding.

Interestingly enough, the paradigmatic story of psychoanalytical theory, the Oedipus tale, has been reinterpreted by the Kleinian school in a way that illustrates this idea of an attack on reason. The traditional psychoanalytical understanding of the Oedipus story concentrates on the sexual desire of the boy for the mother and his hatred of the father, seen as his rival. The story is meant to clarify how this desire and this hatred must be overcome in order for the child to become an adult capable of his own object choices, that is, capable of knowledge and judgement. For psychoanalysis, the type of object choice of an adult is influenced by the resolution of the Oedipus complex. Within this understanding of the story, the emphasis is on the sexual desire for one parent and the hostile, deadly wishes towards the rival parent, which must be relinquished if the child is to grow up as an autonomous adult. In a sense, the resolution of the Oedipus complex marks the entrance of the child, still dominated by its omnipotent wishes, into the world of adult society, ruled by the reality principle. The resolution of the Oedipus complex involves accepting a less immediate (and less omnipotent) but possibly more satisfying gratification. The child cannot kill the father and have the mother, therefore he will become a father himself. The acceptance of the reality principle over the pleasure principle is what marks the socialization of the individual and enables him to find some degree of autonomy and happiness. Without giving up this original understanding, which privileges the sexual desires of the child, contemporary Kleinians have drawn our attention to the deadly wish to destroy knowledge as the real tragedy of Oedipus.

John Steiner, a contemporary Kleinian, has reread the Oedipus myth, adding a second layer to Freud's reading. For him, Oedipus – and Thebes – *should have known* who the man at the crossroads was, and, moreover, *should have known* that the son was desiring and marrying his own mother. Oedipus (the riddle-solver!) had been given the means, by the oracle, to understand what was happening. Surely the people in Thebes knew what was happening. Oedipus should have used his mind and his eyes to see. The tragedy of Oedipus is that he 'turned a blind eye', that is, he chose not to see, he chose not to know. Thus, the tale is not just the story of the tragedy that follows the fulfilment of our infantile wishes; the tragedy is also about the power of our *not wanting to know*, the pull of turning our backs on knowledge whilst looking for the truth. When he realizes what he has done, Oedipus tears out his eyes in despair, devastated by his failure to use them to see.[91] For Steiner, the Oedipus myth is not simply the story of a desire which must be given up, for, if fulfilled, it must lead to tragedy. The story makes us realize that there is in our souls a deep and deadly wish for non-thinking and not-knowing. Our capacity for making links and for knowing is under attack from a drive as powerful as the sexual drive, and this instinct distorts our understanding of reality. The Kleinians postulate as a fundamental component of mental life the death instinct, that is, the envious and destructive attacks which, from the very beginning of life, endanger our good objects and, in so doing, threaten our capacity for making links, in other words, our capacity for seeing and knowing.

This view has raised objections among psychoanalysts and we shall discuss it in more detail in the next chapter. For the moment, it is sufficient to mention in which ways these views can contribute to a modernist understanding of rationality. After all, the Kleinian approach has produced a radical change in psychoanalytical metapsychology, from an isolated subject to a subjectivity which is recognized as relational from the onset of life. As we argued before, Kleinian and object-relations theories made the linguistic turn in psychoanalysis, in so far as they recognized the relevance and the consequences of understanding the mental world as an intersubjective one. This move also stressed how these relations, embedded in our bodily desires and their mental counterparts, are marked by a destructive component that attacks our capacity for knowing and understanding ourselves as inter-related subjects. This perspective recognizes that knowledge and thinking, as encompassing the mental world of unconscious fantasies and relations with others, can become non-thinking: what Bion called minus K, that is, an attack on knowledge. In terms of our purposes here, this could be a fundamental contribution to a modernist discursive theory of truth and ethics, as it can produce an understanding of what, unknown to us and against our best interests, might systematically distort knowledge.

As we mentioned before, this was a central question for Habermas, though he has now abandoned the framework of psychoanalysis as a basis for its explora-tion.[92] A return to psychoanalysis, however, might greatly contribute to an under-standing of what might attack understanding. Lyotard rightly emphasizes the world of the 'other' of reason. Habermas, fearing the mysticism and relativism of such a position, relinquishes to the postmodernist camp that which is fundamentally a modernist argument: the recognition of the unknown as an achievement of reason.

Contemporary Kleinian psychoanalysis provides two central ideas for a modernist defence of rationality. Firstly, it emphasizes the intersubjective dimension of mental life, that is, how I am (or how I can be) in me and in others. In other words, it shows how the boundaries between our internal and external worlds are delineated according to our experiences of our relations with others. Secondly, psychoanalysis also provides us with an insight into the power of our (unconscious) wishes to destroy and attack that which is a universal goal implicit in our communicative life: truth, justice and freedom.

The first point is fundamental to our understanding of ethics, as we can see that the maintenance of right and intersubjective norms is fundamental to our personal happiness. A mature autonomous individual is one who does not require an excessive use of projections, as he or she is able to take full responsibility and care for his or her objects (that is the other subjects he or she relates to). Of course, this is a recognition of the 'other' as a being distinct from a mere repository of our unwanted fantasies. In this sense, autonomy, for Kleinian psychoanalysis, is interwoven with solidarity. The second point – the recognition of the death instinct as part of our mental make-up – allows for an understanding of how, despite its centrality, we can attack and destroy a wish to know and live justly and freely. Without this recognition, the idea of rationality as conscious consensus can, as Lyotard suspects, appear naïve and limited.

The story of knowledge attacked and regained is a complex one. Habermas's view of psychoanalysis focuses on the cognitive process undergone by the patient, with the help of the analyst, in order to regain an understanding of his or her own estranged inner territory.[93] The point argued before is that, for Freud (and Klein), this process involves a working-through of one's mental life, understood as more than a cognitive process. Indeed, our view of what cognition is must change, in order to allow for such a process to take place. The contribution of Kleinian theory is precisely at this level of what we can understand by knowledge, and how entrenched our desire not to know might be. The tragedy of Oedipus, the great riddle-solver, was that *he should have known*. It takes a change of emphasis and perspective, however, to see the story this way, and it is this change in the way of looking at things that allows us to see. This 'change', as Wittgenstein remarked, is not merely a switch from theoretical perspectives; it is more akin to a general, overall Gestalt change that allows us to see the duck rather than the rabbit in the same drawing. Kuhn spoke about it in terms of a 'paradigm' change,[94] and Wittgenstein made famous this style of philosophy that is more concerned with effecting such a change rather than convincing us of the way things are (he was 'showing' rather than 'saying'). This idea that one needs to change in order to see (rather than to see in order to change) is Wittgenstein's idea of philosophy as 'therapy'.[95] What Freud argued in his paper on 'Working Through'[96] was that psychoanalytical knowledge is not abstract cognition, but involves an emotional rearrangement which acknowledges the unconscious dimension of our mental life.

What the Kleinians emphasize is the power of a certain psychic organization to stop us from seeing and knowing. Without an understanding of this power and of its unconscious dimension, we cannot appreciate the tragedy of Oedipus as consisting of the turning of a blind eye. The tragedy is that we are relying on our capacity for thinking to understand what is happening when what is happening stops us from thinking.

When Lyotard talks about that which cannot be said, he is particularly interested in that which cannot be remembered, because the very memory of the repression has been forgotten. According to Freud, repression is not an exclusive mechanism of the Pcs-Cs system. It might be part of the unconscious system and therefore be inaccessible to conscious remembrance. Indeed this is the paradigm of any reign of terror, a world where the memory of past horrors is forever forbidden. This is not, however, the whole story of reason, as reason is also the means of remembering and even constructing (psychoanalytical) concepts such as the unconscious in order to recover the means of thinking about what cannot be thought. The idealization of madness can silence us as powerfully as the forces of (rational) repression, and, moreover, it overlooks the fact that the unconscious is also a locus of repression and violence. It is the articulation of the conscious–preconscious with the unconscious that causes laughter and wonder.

For Lyotard, a critique of totalitarianism has to produce a reflection on the 'immemorial', that is, on that which must not be forgotten but which, when remembered and represented, loses its particular significance. For him, the task of art and avant-garde is precisely that of testifying, without transforming the unique event into 'something to be remembered'. Adorno had already spoken about this paradox, but felt, despairingly, after Auschwitz, that art had become impossible. Lyotard's remarks follow in that path. His distrust of reason makes him explore ways of exposing the deadness of reason.

The seemingly absurd position of denying the Holocaust exemplifies this particular tendency of reason. Generally, we do not engage with the critics of the Holocaust who argue that there were no gas chambers. There is, however, a particularly revealing logic in such denial. The argument says that gas chambers to kill all Jews and dissidents could not have existed because, if they had, no Jews nor any dissidents could testify to such crime (they would all be dead). If they do testify, as indeed they do, they must be liars. The fascination of this type of thinking lies in the way it exposes a very familiar logic, used by twentieth century totalitarian regimes as a justification for genocide. At its core is the idea of a monstrous deed which would be done so perfectly, so thoroughly, that no vestiges of the atrocity would remain. In language, in memory and in thought, there would be no trace, no knowledge of the horror. The atrocity thus gains another dimension: added to the horror of the crime committed is the violence of the erasure of the memory, an erasure that erases itself.

This particular type of logic is quite obvious in the case of the Holocaust and quite vivid in our memories as we recall too the silence that surrounded the crimes committed in the name of the proletariat. It is still present in the reality of the genocides of today. For Lyotard, this is the logic of the 'Grand Narrative' of modernity, a narrative best epitomized by the dream of scientific knowledge. The idea of a narrative that proposes to establish universal criteria to judge all other possible stories, thus establishing the ultimate truth about all possible objects, is a scientific dream out of control, though one that we easily recognize. Ironically, the attempt to produce such a narrative distorts the very idea of truth, as it offers the perfect framework for the repression and demise of any voices which speak differently.

Scientific narratives promote the idea of a discourse without speakers, a transparent language spoken without a context, where narrators without addressees would be telling the truth, based on real facts, independently of the interactions performed. This flattening of reality into an unidimensional story is, of course, a tale of terror and oppression. Habermas spoke about it in terms of the colonization of the lifeworld by the expertise and efficiency of technocratic knowledge.[97] As Lyotard correctly points out, the violence is also the erasure of the memory of language being spoken and fought over conflicting voices attempting to emit, and sometimes succeeding in emitting what seems, for a while, to be a consensual opinion, only to fragment later and give rise to other possible voices. Somehow we seem to have forgotten that there are other possible narratives, other ways of telling the stories. In *The Postmodern Condition*, Lyotard gives the example of the Cashinahua narrative which incorporates the retelling of the story by various members of the culture as part of the tale itself. The fact that the tale is retold and changed across the generations gives the narrative its specific power. The beating of time that can be heard in this way is part of the pleasure of the narrative. Probably the closest we can come to it in our Western cultures, so mesmerized by universal narratives seemingly without narrators, is through children's nursery rhymes. Indeed, these apparently nonsensical song-verses are best appreciated when we open up to the 'immemorial beating' that still plays through them, rather than when we look for a 'story' in their tales.[98]

For Lyotard, the move towards language is the opportunity to exhibit, in language, the various games performed, and to show how rules and their interpretation belong to the game. Therefore they can be, and generally are, fought over as part of what is at stake (*l'enjeu*) in the game. The idea of rules as something beyond or outside the game, grounding it and giving it legitimacy, promotes the idea of a story to end all other possible stories.

Lyotard's opponent, however, should not be modernity. The idea of a 'modern' time, as Baudelaire made clear, is the awareness of time, of a newness that itself aspires to be renewed. Modernity is not a scientific discourse with an aspiration to universal norms that would, in the end, erase time and memory. The modernist dilemma is not how to disguise the particularity and temporality of norms. The real dilemma of modernity is how to produce norms or judgements that have any meaning as universal norms, given that modernity, as a consciousness of time, is also the recognition that there are no last judgements. Every time we judge, we judge a particular case. What modernity as a consciousness implies is that every time we judge, we must assume an aspiration to universalism, as part of the dilemma of reason.[99] Of course, we know that such a task is never fully achieved and remains always to be pursued. According to Habermas, without the striving for the universal, the very idea of a justice that must constantly be re-invented is at risk. Or, as Baudelaire reminds us, without the quest for the absolute, the ever new becomes banal and the same.

The modernist and the postmodernist agree that scientific knowledge does not offer grounds for solving the central question of norms and judgement. They also acknowledge that language, as an intersubjective practice, shifts the emphasis from truth to a moral understanding of a shared background of mutual expectations. Language as a repository of possible forms of life becomes an ethical experience which sustains our sense of justice, freedom and truth. It is here that the main disagreement between the positions of Habermas and Lyotard lies. For Habermas, the recognition of the mutual expectations that form the possibility of communication as understanding leads him to think of the intersubjective world as one of speakers who share an ideal of understanding. Lyotard radically questions this sense of identity, stressing the never-resolved conflicts, differences and disputes that constitute the precarious identities of speakers in language.

Habermas's move towards language effectively shifted the emphasis from a monological subject to an intersubjective world. He has been able, on this basis, to pursue a theory of justice that aims at the autonomy of the individual, whilst recognizing that this freedom can only survive in a world that preserves solidarity amongst autonomous subjects. It is not just the recognition that I will unto others what I will unto myself, and the wish to generalize this will to embrace all possible subjects. The linguistic turn is the fundamental recognition that solidarity *between* subjects is what grounds the possibility of my freedom as an individual. The validity basis of speech is the recognition of this intersubjectivity, as displayed by the mutual expectations of rational justification, and this intersubjectivity promotes an ideal of freedom as autonomy *and* solidarity. As an ideal of language, however, it is based on one of symmetry between speakers (symmetry of opportunities, roles and behaviour) and of transparency within one's own inner world. The problem here is not so much the status of this ideal, whether as an empirical or as *a quasi* transcendental illusion. What is being questioned is the (counterfactual) ideal of a world of symmetry and transparency, as it does not allow for an understanding of the unconscious projections, introjections and fantasies that constitute our actual worlds, internal, external and social. Lyotard is more able to understand the inherent conflict between the worlds of pleasure and pain, conscious and unconscious fantasies, reason and unreason. He is also more aware of how these conflicts shape our fragile sense of identity and difference from others. Psychoanalysis argues, or more precisely, Kleinian object-relations theories argues, in theory and in practice, that our sense of separateness and individuality is constituted by our relationship to others. It is not just that the infant is not separate from the breast to start with. It is that the infant, in being part of the mother, that is, in (necessary) identification with the mother, is also relating to her. To communicate is also to be with the other 'outside' of ourselves. As it learns to separate from the breast, the child gains a sense of identity by internalizing or introjecting the good and bad objects it has been communicating with and projecting onto. Being alone is being able to relate to others in the external world,[100] and this relationship is inextricably bound up with our internal relations to fantasized objects, how we deal with our projections, introjections and splitting off of our unwanted or difficult parts. It is learning to live with and looking after the internal/external objects (subjects) that make us into ourselves.

What postmodernity can give us is not so much the discovery of individual particularities and the refusal of universals in a world of only relative values. What postmodernity can give us, and indeed Lyotard does, is a stress on the world of language as one of agonistic relations, where no stake is decided beforehand and where identities are constantly being fought over. This postmodern insight is, of course, the recognition of the radical alterity of the 'other' and, most importantly, the recognition of this radical alterity within oneself. This insight should not endanger the project of modernity as the recognition of the rational and ethical dimensions displayed in language. But this recognition of intersubjectivity has to allow for that which we do not know as maybe something radically different from what is known. This is an insight that Habermas has dropped, together with his lost interest in psychoanalysis.

This dichotomy, that is, the impossibility of knowledge and the striving for understanding all the same, is part of modernity. Habermas's theory of communication has come too close to an actual repression and negation of the unknown, under the guise of equality as identity. Lyotard, on the other hand, is too prone to an attack on knowledge as totalitarianism and to an idealization of the unknown as more real than understanding. It is between these two poles, the postmodern reduction of reason to violence and the modernist repression of the unknown, that, to use Habermas's beautiful image, the 'unavoidable illusion' of justice lies. Language is conflict and understanding, the known and the unknown, what is said and what cannot be articulated. Without this understanding, the idea of an ethics that effectively moves to a dialogical, relational intersubjectivity fails, for the 'other' becomes the self and the same. Language is not the multiplication of the same; it is the acknowledgement and mutual recognition of the difference and radical alterity of the 'other', both in the 'other' and within oneself.

4

FREUD AND KLEIN

One of the central arguments of this book is that the way psychoanalysis intro-
duces and develops the idea of the unconscious is particularly helpful to a discussion of rationality. Up to this chapter, we have used psychoanalysis to expose the
limitations of the thoughts of Habermas and Lyotard as to what reason is not. A
philosophical overview of certain points in the work of Freud and Melanie Klein
could contribute to our discussion on reason and interpretation. This is not, and in
such a short space could not be, a detailed presentation of their work. Nonetheless,
the development of the concept of the unconscious in Freud is particularly interesting. For, as we shall see, as Freud changes his approach to the unconscious from a
topographical localization to a part of a complex structure of personalizations of
the mind, his understanding of psychoanalysis changes as well. What had started
as a scientistic model of the mind, a hydraulic machine seeking to balance different
forces, becomes the more mythical and metaphysical battle between life and death.
Psychoanalysis moves from a scientistic ideal towards a hermeneutic model of
interpretation.

What leads Freud to this change is not the conflict between an unconscious ruled
by the pleasure principle and a rational ego trying, in the name of reality, to over-
power the instinctual libidinal demands. For Freud, what lie beyond the pleasure
principle are death and aggression. The battle is not between Eros and Ananke, the
libidinal sexual instincts facing reality or necessity, but between Eros and
Thanatos, life and death. The 'other' of reason should not be idealized as desire, as
pure instinctual life, for it harbours in its core a threat to life itself. Melanie Klein is
the author who took this controversial development of Freud's theory most seriously. Indeed, by concentrating on the death instinct, she was able to show how,
from the very start, the infants are struggling with their destructive as well as their
libidinal instincts. We intend to show the particular relevance of Kleinian psychoanalysis to philosophy and the human sciences.

One of the most contentious issues in the interpretation of Freud is the question
of how much of a natural scientist he was and to what extent he thought of himself
as creating a new type of science. There is telling evidence both ways. It is under-
standable that, as a medical doctor, with a particular interest in neurophysiology,
he should hope, one way or the other, to read the new psychic phenomena from

within this perspective. On the other hand, as Freud himself commented in his autobiography, his real concern had always been with cultural and human problems and, in this sense, he was much closer to philosophy than to science.[101] From a philosophical point of view, there is no doubt that one of Freud's great contributions is precisely his need – willing or unwilling – to invent ways of thinking about a type of phenomenon which was itself new and which, he claimed, had a meaning. Habermas locates Freud's great creative moment as the time when he stopped working with hypotheses borrowed from the natural sciences (treatment via hypnosis) and created the idea of a talking cure. In Habermasian terms, Freud was seeking to restore, through communicative interaction, a meaning that had been lost (repeating, remembering and working through).

Some commentators have suggested that the choice of Greek and Latin words for the English translation of the Freudian concepts (cathexis, ego, id, etc.), was meant to give the new discipline a scientific credibility. This choice might have steered the (English) reception of the new science too much in the direction of a scientistic reading which did not, in fact, do justice to the German original. Indeed, the colloquialism of Freud's choice of words (Ich, Überich, Es) would suggest a more hermeneutic approach to the meaning of psychic phenomena.[102] This type of argument is subject to many readings, as recent debates surrounding the new translation of the Standard Edition have shown. Some more conservative commentators, trying to restore Freud to the natural sciences' fold, have argued the opposite, namely that the established German natural sciences' tradition in Freud's time favoured this type of colloquialism when creating new medical concepts.

Ricoeur's reading stresses the *tension* between these two currents in Freud's thought. There are, he argues, two discourses in Freud's work: the energetic and the hermeneutic. The energetic discourse emphasizes the organic dimension of psychic life, using the metaphor of the organism as a hydraulic machine, imported from the natural sciences, to describe psychic phenomena. In this view, the main aim of the (psychic) organism is to discharge any excess energy and to maintain at the lowest possible level any unpleasurable increase in excitation. The organism is thus ruled by the principle of constancy which seeks to maintain an equilibrium between the various charges and discharges. This model is at its strongest in the early *Project for a Scientific Psychology* (1895). There, the human mind is a battlefield of conflicting forces, ruled by the principle of constancy. The weight of this scientistic metaphor, so embedded in the German scientific tradition of Mayer and Helmholtz,[103] is present throughout Freud's work. In the 1915 paper 'The Unconscious', Freud is still lamenting his failure to establish a physiological basis for his psychological explanations, saying that he had given up 'for the present' his hope of linking psychology with anatomy.[104]

The concept of drive or instinct[105] as an internal stimulus invested with or cathected by a certain amount of libidinal energy and seeking to discharge any excess, belongs to this framework, as does the Freudian idea of an organism ruled by the pleasure–unpleasure principle. Unpleasure is associated with an increase in the amount of stimulation and pleasure with a decrease. The introduction of the reality principle in no way challenges this model, which remains faithful to the idea that the aim of the organism is to maintain as low as possible the level of stimulation. The reality principle constitutes the process through which we learn to delay the satisfaction of pleasure, still conceived of as the lowering of excitation, and to tolerate unpleasure, the excess energy.

Hermeneutic discourse, on the other hand, privileges the level of *meaning* of conscious and unconscious life. Freud's choice of title for his magnum opus, *The Interpretation* (and not the science) *of Dreams* shows him clearly opting for the hermeneutic discourse, that is, opting for the need to understand the meaning of psychic phenomena through interpretation. A hermeneutic discourse establishes links between meanings, and not between language and the things themselves. An interpretation is not a compilation of references to fixed meanings, notwithstanding the popular manuals of 'dream solving'. There is, of course, in Freud, the recognition of a social and cultural repertory of symbols for sexual parts and thoughts, and we undoubtedly use this language in dreams when we need to express forbidden, repressed thoughts in a disguised way. Nevertheless, the interpretation of dreams goes beyond this 'dictionary' compilation (though, once again, a dictionary is the explanation of meaning through other meanings). A dream is a narrative (the dream work), and it is remembered and retold in another narrative, which bears the erasures of repression. The associations that this telling elicits in the patient (and in the analyst) are part of this narrative and it is only through these interwoven narratives that an interpretation of the dream as a wish fulfilment becomes possible. This is not the reduction of meaning to an organic or physical reality, even if we conceive of this final 'reality' as a wish, for these wishes are, once again, *narratives* that express conflicting aspects of a dynamic psyche.

It could still be argued that there is a reductionism in Freud's work, in so far as he attempts to find the child in the adult, that is, to show how our early childhood experiences determine and shape our adult capacities, and this is indeed correct. Then this argument could be extended to a claim that a regression to a primal scene might give the keys to the meaning of the later symptom. There is ample evidence in Freud to support this view, made very popular in books and films in the 1950s and 1960s.[106] What Ricoeur and hermeneutic philosophy emphasize is that the primal scene, the childhood memories, the dream, the trauma and the symptom are narratives, that is, that they are, and must be, expressed in language. This recognition does not lead to the idea that if we cannot find an ultimate, primal event, then everything becomes a story among other stories, mere tales with no truth content. In psychoanalysis there is a truth to be gained by remembering and working through, but this is a work within language, an opening up to the various levels of meaning embedded in our practices. This, as discussed in the previous chapters, is a particularly difficult insight for it seems to open up the abyss of relativism and scepticism right in front of our very eyes.

This is not necessarily so. An example of the use of this insight can be seen in the Kleinian practice of analysing what the patient does – in the here and now of the session – with his or her memories.[107] In other words, what the patient says should not blind us to *how* it is told, that is (remembering J. L. Austin), to what he does in saying what he says. The memory constitutes a certain choice of story, organized in a certain way, with a view to evoke certain feelings and responses in the patient and the analyst. The awareness of the various levels of meaning of our memories, our symptoms, our dreams and our stories is extremely important for understanding the meaning of the re-enactment of the past in the present. The past can only exist in the present. This does not mean that the past does not exist; rather, this approach invites us to look at what is being done in the present by remembering a certain past. Undoubtedly, we do what we do by telling what we tell as an endless repetition and reworking of a certain personal history that needs to be re-enacted. Nevertheless, our histories exist in the present, in the ways in which we tell and remember our past and, as such, they are open to understanding and interpretation. There is no primal, final truth to be revealed, or, as Ricoeur puts it, '... analysis has not led us from the less to the better known'.[108]

For Ricoeur, what is told is also what is and will remain absent. This absence will not be replaced by a full knowledge that explains and dissipates the initial enigma. It is an absence that makes the enigma meaningful. The idea, for instance, that the childhood memory of Leonardo is what explains the smile of the Gioconda, is a clear example of this type of psychoanalytical reductionism. Ricoeur challenges it by showing that Freud sees in Leonardo's painting not only the infantile wishes for the mother, but *his overcoming of them through art*. In fact, his infantile wishes can only be perceived through the nostalgic beauty of the smile which suggests the infantile longings already overcome and disavowed, present in their absence.[109] Art and analysis create the possibility of new ways of talking about the absence rather than the real fulfilment or exact description of a given event, brought back from the past.

Another way of grasping the hermeneutic weight, or the emphasis on meaning in Freud's work is to look at his concept of instinct, the somatic force that rules our psychic life. Even instinct is not a purely somatic force. For Freud, the libidinal instinct (and the term 'libido' goes beyond a purely energetic account of the instinct) 'lies in the frontier between the mental and the physical'.[110] The instinct has its source in the organism which generates the tension, but it also has an aim (satisfaction through a discharge of energy) and an object to which it becomes attached. An instinct must have a psychic presentation (which might be unconscious), however, as, without it, it cannot reach its aim. The psychic representations of the presentation of the instinct are what enable us to talk about and possibly know the instincts. It makes no sense to speak of instinct in purely energetic terms. To reduce the psychic presentation to the somatic stratum is absurd. On the other hand, to forget that there is something beyond the psychic presentation is to miss the point and the impact of Freud's work.

Ricoeur's reading of Freud warns us against the dangers of trying to 'improve' Freud by updating what might be seen as outdated scientific ideals. Ricoeur's hermeneutic reading takes the energetic model seriously, as a necessary metaphor for what the discourse on meaning *cannot know or say*, as in saying it, we would be moving from the level of force to the level of meaning. Without the energetic hypothesis, the discourse on meaning loses its particular strength. Conversely, the level of force can only exist through meaning, as an instinct cannot exist without its presentation. Thus, Ricoeur claims that to be faithful to the psychoanalytical spirit is 'not by defending its scientific myth as science but by interpreting it as a myth'.[111] In this sense, psychoanalysis is not purely hermeneutic, as Ricoeur makes clear in a later paper (1973), as it attempts to understand and explain a deeper structure of meaning.[112]

The scientistic wish to resolve the conflict and to reduce meaning to force is quite powerful, and its pull is felt throughout Freud's work. Ricoeur's point is that, towards the end of his life, Freud moved to a more 'romantic' position, finally departing from a scientific conception of the human psyche. Most Freudian commentators[113] agree that there was a move from a scientistic to a hermeneutic model of the mind, when he moved from his first model (Conscious-Preconscious and Unconscious) to his second (Id, Ego and Superego). There is, however, more controversy surrounding the introduction of the death instinct and its relevance to psychoanalysis. Ricoeur's reading of Freud emphasizes that what lies *Beyond The Pleasure Principle* (1920) is not reality or necessity, but the death instinct. For him, it is at this moment that psychoanalysis finally comes into its own and achieves its independent discourse. This is a major claim, and in order to understand its full impact, it is important to follow what happened between *Project* and *Beyond the Pleasure Principle*. Melanie Klein, for very different reasons and from a different background, would have agreed with Ricoeur's view on the significance of the death instinct.

Freud's work at first attempted to understand the psychic apparatus by creating a topographic model which suggested that there were two levels of the mind. Between the first, the conscious-preconscious or the perception-consciousness system (Pcpt-Cs)[114] and the second, the unconscious (Ucs), lay the frontier-zone of censorship. For Freud, the unconscious was that which was outside, indeed barred from consciousness, but still capable of expressing itself in consciousness. The two systems were intrinsically related, with the unconscious trying to push itself into consciousness in distorted, compromised forms, whereas consciousness tried, in the name of the self-preservation of the individual, to repress and control, never with complete success, these unconscious thrusts. In spite of their dynamic character, Freud was thinking of these systems in a topographical manner, as his metaphor of the mind as composed of chambers and antechambers guarded by the censorship of a doorkeeper, made clear.[115]

For many, this approach to the unconscious meant the decentring of the subject, in the sense that meaning was no longer to be found in the conscious 'I' of the person, but outside it, in the regions of the unconscious libidinal impulses. The repression exercised on this unconscious by the ego could then be seen as the overpowering and repression of the pure sexual desire, which was the source of meaning in the organism. The Freudian picture is, however, much more complex. The 'decentring' of the subject brought about by psychoanalysis is not just a relocation of the source of truth in a different area, a transposition to another region of the same conception of an 'I' and of truth and reflection, but a radical rethinking of what this 'I' and of what reason can be.

Freud did not remain restricted to his anatomico-geographical approach, for he developed the economic and dynamic characteristics of these systems as well. Indeed, in the unconscious, the energy flows freely, following its own rules of condensation and displacement, where one thing can be both itself and its opposite (primary process). This system is ruled by the principle of pleasure which demands immediate satisfaction (the lowering of the stimulation). In the case of the conscious-preconscious system, the energy flows in a more controlled manner and thus allows for the development of rational thought, which follows the logic of non-contradiction (secondary process).[116] This system is ruled by the reality principle which can delay satisfaction, thereby expanding thought and creating new possibilities for the release of energy.

It could be said that the two systems are basically in conflict. The demands of the unconscious instinctual organism have to be curbed by a conscious ego which, as the receptor of the stimuli and of information concerning reality, is better adapted for survival. Seen in these terms, there are two systems (Pcpt-Cs and Ucs), two modes of functioning (pleasure and reality principles, primary and secondary processes) and two instincts (libidinal and ego-instincts) which are distinct and permanently in conflict. In fact, in spite of the emphasis on the conflict, there is also a continuum between the two systems, or, as Freud puts it, the recognition that reality is not the 'deposition' of the pleasure principle, just its 'safeguarding'.[117] Indeed, as we have already mentioned, the reality principle does not question the mode of functioning of the organism, as it still approaches it as aiming solely to achieve pleasure through a discharge of energy. What it recognizes, however, is the organism's ability to postpone this immediate, but ephemeral, satisfaction in view of attaining a more permanent one.

There were many problems with this first model which became apparent in Freud's development of the idea of ego instincts. These instincts, as opposed to the sexual ones, were geared towards self-preservation. The influence of biology, with its emphasis on the conflict between the needs of the individual and the needs of the species as they face a hostile environment, is visible here.[118] The person is viewed as a living organism ruled by instinctual forces which must be curbed as he or she enters into contact with reality. The person is presumed to be a solitary individual facing external reality. The idea of the individual interrelating with others from the start of life, thereby producing and reproducing a social as well as a biological history, cannot be accounted for here. At this stage, although Freud states that 'instinct' is both a physical and a mental concept, he still views it largely as biological fact. Instinct has a somatic source and an object to enable it to reach satisfaction, but this object is, in a way, still in the background, with instinctual force taking centre stage. The recognition of the role of the object comes about with the introduction of narcissism, that is, the idea that the person itself can be an object to the instinct. Then the questions regarding the role and meaning of culture in this struggle for survival of the individual and the species can begin to be addressed [119]. But first, the original system had to be rethought.

Freud had argued that there were two basic instincts: the libidinal (sexual) and the ego (self-preservation) instincts. There was the problem of explaining where the energy of the latter came from. Freud had argued that it derived from the sexual instincts, which originally directed the libidinal energy towards the body, and then towards the ego as a unified image of the body. This created a 'reservoir of libido' [120] that could then be used by the ego-instincts as they sought their objects for self-preservation (food, for instance). The image of the reservoir pictured the ego as a locus of dammed-up instinctual energy, and not merely as a place through which energy passed. This differentiation of the two sources of energy harboured an implicit ambiguity, for the ego was conceived of as both the source and the object of instinctual energy. [121] With the introduction of narcissism, this problem became even more clear, leading to a reformulation of the systems that constituted the mind.

The idea of narcissism gives recognition to the possibility that the ego can be itself an object of desire, as in the case of auto-eroticism or of a baby discovering itself and its body, as we mentioned earlier. It also goes further, as Freud recognized that libidinal impulses can be redirected to the ego at later stages and as part of normal sexual development. Narcissism, then, is not restricted to an original pool or reservoir of the libido, nor is it a feature of early forms of sexuality and/or of perverse and pathological modes of functioning.

The first point to be noted is that the introduction of narcissism changes the approach to instinct from one of emphasis on the biological impulse directed towards an external object. It now becomes the mental process that accompanies the organic drive which takes centre stage as it tells us whether the instinct is directed towards an external object or towards the ego. In other words, the emphasis now is on the type of object choice made at the various stages of sexual development. O. Mannoni commented that this transition period effected a move from an economy of instincts to an 'economy of desire'. [122] Here the ego has become both the subject of the *cogito* and the object of desire. In fact, with the introduction of narcissism, Freud is really saying that the ego becomes the subject of the *cogito by virtue of being* the object of desire.

Narcissism stresses the role of the mental representations of the instinct and how they create objects for instinctual satisfaction, including the ego itself. These mental representations or fantasies actually determine and colour much of our life as human beings, in so far as they are ways of relating to the world as well as providing the possibility of the satisfaction of an instinctual force. For instance, depending on the various phases of sexual development, the libidinal instinct has as its source the mouth, the anus or the phallus. Feeding, defecating and copulating satisfy basic needs, thus satisfying a libidinal instinct, a satisfaction which provokes pleasure and defines a way of relating to objects in the external world. Thus, we incorporate food or retain and expel faeces, but we also 'devour' a book, 'drink' words, incorporate knowledge, spoil and soil what we hate, etc. These are not simply metaphors; they define an imaginary world embedded in instinctual life which is never purely physical. The introduction of narcissism acknowledges this world of fantasies and how important they are for our object choices. Thus, a narcissistic choice makes a man love in the other what he is himself, what he was, what he would like to be or someone that he feels is part of himself. Or an anaclitic (non-narcissistic) attachment type of choice makes him seek in the object of love the woman who feeds him or the man who protects him.[123]

The second point to be noted is that this approach changes the way we conceive of the subject and the object of desire. Narcissism shows how the libido which was directed towards external objects is redirected towards the ego, and how, in the process, an *internal* object is created and becomes the object of the libido. This becomes quite apparent in the process of mourning and in melancholia. The continuous self-criticisms that follow the loss of a loved object show that the identification with the dead object is redirected towards oneself. The complaints directed at the object ('Why have you left me?') are reintrojected as self-criticisms ('I am no good, I do not deserve to be loved.'). This led Freud to a completely novel way of thinking about the subject and the object of desire as formed within this interplay of projections, introjections and identifications.

For Freud, identification is the most primitive form of attachment to another person, and it follows the mechanisms of the oral phase, when the object desired is eaten or devoured and an internal object is created in our internal world (introjection).[124] There are later forms of identification, such as the one present in the resolution of the Oedipus complex. In this later case, the child wishes to have the mother, but it also wishes to *be* like the mother or the father, irrespective of its sexual desires.

The problem of identification is, in fact, one of the most complex ones in psychoanalytical theory, as it is the introjection of the desired object that creates the identification with it, and, moreover, as the Oedipus complex shows and as Ricoeur stresses, this introjection and identification are not necessarily always sexual in origin.[125] These are very difficult problems which we shall not develop here. It is important to note, however, what consequences this approach has for an understanding of the mind, as what is being talked about, with this emphasis on identification and introjection, is how mechanisms of identity and mutual comprehension are established from the very early moments of life. Freud is no longer restricted to the view that the organism is seeking the purely physical satisfaction of the instinct. There is a recognition of the communication established, from the very early moments of life, such as, say, those of a baby feeding from the breast. The mother provides more than milk, even more than warmth and love; through the complex identifications and introjections that are taking place, the mother–baby relationship creates a space of mutual understanding. This is a central point for Kleinian theory, as we shall see later, for Klein and her followers argue that feeding is a fundamental experience not just in terms of pleasure and of the satisfaction of a need, but also in terms of setting the grounds for the principles of a moral and social world.

Freud's second model of the mind provides a different mode of understanding the three instances of the mind. It is not just a matter of saying that the ego, the id and the superego do not correspond exactly to the conscious and the unconscious topographical locations of the first model, though this is indeed the case, as a quick look at the largely unconscious defences of the ego shows. It is more a matter of conceiving of the ego in a different way. According to the first model, the ego develops out of the instinctual forces, as a necessary change brought about by the adaptation to reality. In other words, the ego is formed in the encounter with the external world, in view of the survival of the individual and the species. According to the second model, the ego is formed through the processes of identification and introjection with the objects of the instincts, which are the other persons and the way we relate to these persons and their own conscious and unconscious ways of relating to us. The ego is formed by identifications with the other, through the images of the other in oneself as seen through the eyes of the other, a process that Lacan famously called the 'mirror' stage. Needless to say, we do not relate as fully conscious beings to fully integrated subjects, but we relate to others through our internal world of object-relations, which influences not just the choice of external objects but also constitutes our own ego and our ego-ideal. This is a very different approach from that of Freud's first model of the mind, for it is an intersubjective, interhuman world (the identifications, projections and introjections) which constitutes the ego and the ego-ideal rather than exposure to an external reality outside these relations. The idea of a subject and an object have to be conceived from within this internalized intersubjective world of object-relations which makes possible a relation to the environment. As Laplanche and Pontalis summarize, 'instead of the ego being seen as an apparatus whose development starts from the system Pcpt-Cs, it becomes an internal formation originating from certain privileged perceptions which derive not from the external world in general but specifically from the interhuman world.'[126]

The second approach to the mind, heralded by the introduction of narcissism and configurated in *The Ego and the Id*, is structural rather than geographical. The unconscious is no longer that which lies outside consciousness. Inside and outside, external and internal, have become distinctions made possible by human interrelations rather than by pre-existing realities. The ego, the id and the superego are better understood as possible 'personalizations' of the 'I', as anonymous (id), as a real person in the real world (ego), and as the moral idea or the sublime (the superego). All these instances have both conscious and unconscious dimensions. In this way, it is not just the neurotic who, to paraphrase Freud, is not the master in his own house. The social being and the ethical man are *also* conscious and unconscious and therefore subject to the same type of conflicts as the neurotic, which means, in other words, that they can be as narcissistically resistant to facing their problems as the neurotic individual subject. For, as we shall see, narcissism is the real 'evil genius'[127] that distorts and resists the truth. If we think of Descartes, the evil genius was there at his starting-point. Indeed, to start reflection by retreating into oneself is to presume both too much and too little, to attribute to solitary reflection capacities that it does not have and to deny the mutual bonds of dependency, language and culture that must pre-exist for reflection to take place. Even the purest of motives, for example, the quest for truth, can be distorted by narcissism and omnipotence.

Finally, with the new model, Freud can discuss the social and moral dimensions of psychic phenomena. With the introduction of the superego, the ego now faces not just the demands of the libido and of reality, but also the demands of the moral conscience. Indeed, the Oedipus complex reveals the desire of the child for the mother, a desire that will eventually have to be abandoned, out of fear of retaliation by the more powerful father. The resolution of the Oedipus complex involves, on one hand, the giving up of the desire for the mother and, on the other, the identification with an ideal of what the child would like to be as a father or a mother, an identification both with the parent as an ego ideal and with the ego ideal of the parent. In order for the superego to be 'the vehicle of tradition and of all the time-resisting judgements of value which have propagated themselves in this manner from generation to generation',[128] the child's superego has to identify with the parents' own superego, mostly unconscious. Thus, the severity of the superego should not be taken to be a direct result of the actual severity of the parents, which might be very mild, but of their own internal prohibitions. With the resolution of the Oedipus complex comes the entrance into the social and moral arena, for it involves a renunciation of sexual desire *and* an identification with the figure of the parent as a moral conscience which is not libidinal in character.

Usually, the Freudian social and cultural body of work is viewed with enormous suspicion, due to its positivistic traits, so indebted to Comtean-inspired sociology. J. Whitebook,[129] following in the spirit of Ricoeur,[130] was able to disregard this dated character of Freud's scientistic sociology and to read those texts anew as myth. Thus, he was able to show that the most important point of *Totem and Taboo* is that what follows the murder of the father is the pact between the brothers, or, in other words, the beginning of a social order. This can only be done once the brothers relinquish their narcissistic identification with the father, which makes them feel that they should actually *be* the father, entitled to kill the brothers and to have the mother. It is only when this narcissistic identification with the father is given up that society can begin: with the social pact between the brothers.

At an individual level, the resolution of the Oedipus complex brings about an integration of the individual with society, through a renunciation of the libidinal demands and an internalization of the parental prohibitions and demands. This renunciation and internalization can only take place if the child abandons his omnipotent view of himself as capable of satisfying the mother. Growing up into a social world involves a blow to one's narcissism as it involves some level of recognition of one's frailty, dependency and inadequacy. Introjection of the father involves the introjection of both a model of what one wants to become and (some) awareness that in reality one cannot be the omnipotent father of one's infantile fantasies, modelled, of course, on the child's own narcissism. The child has to be like the others and to accept belonging to a community cemented by reciprocal duties and obligations, an insight very close to Habermas's ethical discourse theory.

The superego, then, is the internalization of a complex moral and social figure, though this process is threatened by the problem of narcissism, the individual's difficulty in relinquishing his infantile omnipotence. It is the internalization of both a judge and a model, that is, an identification with what the child wishes to be, but also an internalization of an observant and critical agency that demands that the ego be as good as it wishes to be. Given the narcissistic traits that permeate the ego ideal, these demands can be very harsh indeed.

The superego has a dual aspect. As the proponent of culture, it is the possibility of sublimating and symbolizing loss and pain, of making absence a creative space from which thought can emerge. The much quoted game of Freud's grandson playing with the reel, the Fort-da game, is an example of this sublimating role of culture. It is the mastering, through symbols, play and words, of the unbearable pain of dependency and loss. The superego is also, however, the very cruel and destructive judge who finds everything wanting. This is clearly manifest in neurotic behaviour and in the processes of mourning and melancholia mentioned earlier. It is also a familiar mechanism, as a minute of listening to one's own internal criticisms or a glance at our own deprecatory, derogatory and detached observations of ourselves will make clear.

In fact, the severity and cruelty of the superego, as seen by clinical observation of the power of resistance, sadism and masochism, as well as the death and destruction of the First World War, led Freud to a reformulation of the duality of the instincts. The original duality in terms of ego and libidinal instincts was, in fact, a disguised form of monism, in so far as the ego-instincts were themselves sexual in origin. Moreover, as mentioned earlier, they were also ruled by the pleasure principle, though they followed the more arduous route via reality, which promised a longer-lasting satisfaction. Freud's later view offers two contrasting instincts: the life-asserting instinct and the instinct of death and destruction. The biological, psychological and cultural phenomena forced him to accept that mental processes cannot be 'exclusively governed by the desire for pleasure. These phenomena are unmistakable indications of the presence of a power in mental life which we call the instinct of aggression or of destruction according to its aims, and which we trace back to the original death instinct of living matter.'[131]

This is one of Freud's most controversial developments, one that a great number of his followers do not accept. For Ricoeur, it is a major step in his development and one, in fact, that should be considered as giving rise to a third model of the mind. For him, it is at this moment that psychoanalysis comes into its own, with its own discourse and description of the great forces of life and death. If, before, the mind was formed in the individual's struggle to survive and adapt to 'reality', now the battle was of a different order. Lyotard's reading of Freud (and Marcuse's as well) is stuck in the opposition between instinctual, sexual desire and a repressive ego and superego that express themselves in a culture of death: an unnecessary and even unreasonable battle in our world of plenty.[132] Freud's point is, however, more complex.

With his 'third model', Freud sees the instinctual id as both life and death, both the repository of vital forces and yet also the more difficult to detect and silent wish to attack and to destroy all that fosters life. As far as the ego is concerned, it is simplistic to reduce it simply to a repressive agency. The ego can use reason and insight as tools on the side of Eros – a symbol of that which affirms life – which should not be reduced to sexuality. Indeed, since for Freud sadism and masochism are eroticized versions of the death instinct, it makes no sense to identify Eros and sexuality. On the other hand, the ego is a pool of narcissism, always prone to imagine itself as the grounds and sole source of truth and reason. The difference between reason and rationalization, between truth and its negation, is not easy for the ego to establish by itself. Narcissism leads the ego to deny continually its constitution from an internal world of object-relations, created in the very real interhuman world upon which we all depend. Finally, the superego, the agency which most clearly serves the culture of death through its aggressive and destructive unconscious demands, provides also the possibility of sublimation. Its enormous violence and destructivity, so visible in neurotic behaviour, melancholia and obsessive neurosis, as well as in the negative therapeutic reaction, can also be put to work for the service of life. Culture is repression but it is also sublimation, the creation of a space for symbols to express pain and loss. It can also be a defence against our innate aggression. As Ricoeur puts it, the superego uses internal violence to counter the wish to externalize aggression, and thus, culture becomes the possibility of controlling destruction, by making 'death work against death'. Indeed, if one sees culture as the defence against destruction, one is finally speaking of the most difficult renunciation that culture demands of the individual, which is the renunciation not of the individual's sexuality, but of his aggression. Culture and reason are not opposed to the libido; reason and culture can both work for life or death, by affirming the mutual bonds of dependency and love between individuals that create a community or by fostering the destruction and aggression that also lie within those bonds in various guises.

I do not wish to discuss here the criticisms and problems of Freud's later theory of the mind. Not all of his followers developed his later views. Indeed, some, for instance, the French schools, concentrated on the libidinal dimension of the unconscious ('desire'). Without the death instinct as its counterpart, 'desire' becomes an idealization of the instinct, coloured by a suspicion towards the ego and rational thought which is self-defeating. Psychoanalysis is a rational reflection and it seems doomed to fail if the wish for truth, which must be presumed in order for psychoanalysis to have a meaning, is associated with a repressive and therefore untrustworthy ego. On the other hand, an over-emphasis of the critical powers of the ego, so present in the American tradition of ego-psychology which undoubtedly influenced Habermas, is misleading, when there is no acknowledgement of the narcissistic, omnipotent and destructive deadly aspects of the ego and the superego. The denial of the reciprocal duties and bonds that create the reflexive and moral subject is one possible mistake, but these narcissistic traits can be carried over to an intersubjective ethical discourse as well, as we shall see in the next chapter. In order to understand these consequences, it is very important to turn to Melanie Klein and her school of object-relations theory.

Melanie Klein started her work with very young children, claiming that it was possible to analyze them following the same rigorous principles of Freudian psychoanalytical interpretation as used with adults. To this end, she approached their play as a language, and interpreted it as a form of expressing their mental, unconscious conflicts. This was quite an innovative step, as the accepted approach at the time, as proposed by Anna Freud and her followers, was that a child's ego was too immature before the development of the Oedipus complex to cope with psychoanalytical interpretations. For Anna Freud, the child had not yet developed a superego and therefore required support and encouragement, that is, a pedagogical rather than a psychoanalytical intervention. Klein maintained the same rigorous setting as the one used for the psychoanalysis of adults, though she used toys and play. She interpreted the material according to its urgency, addressing the child's anxieties from the very start.[133]

What Klein found in her clinical experience led her to a radicalization of Freud's theory. In working with children, she found a very cruel form of primitive, pre-Oedipal superego, one which had a paralyzing and destructive effect on their lives. This savage superego, like the 'Fisherwoman' and 'Rubberwoman' of Erna's fantasies,[134] worked in a pre-genital fashion, devouring, biting, soiling and destroying internal objects. Departing from Freud, who claimed that the internalization of guilt came with the resolution of the Oedipus complex at the genital phase, Klein maintained that a more primitive pre-Oedipal situation could be found at a much earlier phase.

When an infant turns to the breast, it looks for the satisfaction of its basic needs: nourishment, affection and pleasure. Given that the mother is generally a 'good enough mother', to use the term coined by Winnicott, the process of growing up into the world should be a smooth and uneventful one. Klein helped us to understand why this is not so by showing how an unconscious world of fantasies is at work from the earliest moments of life.

For her, the infant is, from the start, struggling with its own aggression and anger at its frailty and dependency. The baby wants the breast for itself all the time, as it wishes, when it wishes. The baby wants to *have* the breast, and its failure to do so, which implies a recognition of the separate existence of the mother, provokes enormous feelings of rage, frustration and violence that can actually spoil the good feeding experience when the breast becomes available. This bad experience is then expelled to the 'outside' world (it becomes part of a bad breast which is 'outside'), but, as we are talking here about the fantasies of the baby, it is also part of the baby's own internal mental world. The baby is now scared of possible retaliations from this introjected mental object (the bad breast), which might damage an idealized good object. Given the baby's feelings of omnipotence at this stage, this bad breast can be seen as very bad indeed, thus requiring further splittings and projections, which are inevitably accompanied by the introjections of ferociously cruel part-objects and an over-idealization of the good object.

What Klein was describing here was the very primitive world of mental representations of the instincts, seen as *both* affirmative and destructive of love, and how these representations or fantasies actually shape our perceptions of ourselves and the world we live in. These mental representations of instincts or fantasies are, at this stage, very enmeshed with our bodies and dependent on our bodily ways of relating to the world. Thus, Klein stresses the oral, anal and urethral ways of relating and expressing these fantasies, and how they are both loving and destructive. The baby sucks contentedly but it also bites; it takes in and expels the food, and so forth. The conflict of love and hatred is there, expressed in a form of relating which incorporates the desired object through introjection, or expels it through projections followed by further introjections and projections. The beginnings of guilt are there too. This is not the fully fledged Oedipus complex, which involves a more mature identification and renunciation of the object that is both desired and feared, but these primitive objects shape and set the grounds for the later genital phase.

At this early stage, dominated by omnipotent narcissism, the child desires the riches and the goodness of the mother, felt to be infinite and all too powerful, and wishes to possess them. The destructive attacks on this powerful and desirable object (the mother) are split off, projected and then introjected, forming the beginnings of a very cruel superego which is the result not so much of the repression of libidinal desire but of the guilt (or fear) of the baby's own innate greed and aggression. In a sense, the necessary blow to one's narcissism which accompanies a successful resolution of the Oedipus complex has not yet taken place and therefore the projections and introjections which Klein claims are fundamental to our identities, are much more powerful. The post-Oedipal identification with the parental figures, which accepts the need to belong to a community of peers, is not yet here. At this stage, there is a very harsh and cruel desire to have or to annihilate the object desired.

Although Klein was developing Freud's idea of a conflict between Eros and Thanatos, her own style of writing was very different from his. The tentative and rather speculative quality of Freud's texts relating to the death instinct are not hers. The almost apologetic quality of the reluctance with which Freud accepted the need to postulate the death instinct in order to explain otherwise incomprehensible mental phenomena, is very distant from Klein's papers. Her work, so close to her clinical experience, has an almost concrete quality. The way she talks about bad and good internal objects can be quite off-putting; it seems, at first sight, to be naïve and far-fetched. She talks about a pre-verbal baby as if it were capable of a degree of sophisticated knowledge, which is hard to accept.

To do justice to Klein, however, it is necessary to understand what she was trying to do. She was expanding the psychoanalytical insights into the meaning of psychic phenomena to areas untouched by Freud's theory, and thereby creating a new theory and practice. Indeed, the great contribution of Kleinians is their clinical experience, an experience that has been informed by their extensive practice with very young children, with babies and, in the case of Segal, Rosenfeld and others, with psychotic patients. Their material showed that these 'irrational' beings were all meaningful participants in a communicative interaction, though up until Klein they had not been seen as such. Freud shocked his generation by claiming that children had sexual desires that shaped the meaning of their communication. Klein shocked her peers by claiming that the *infant* had sexual *and* aggressive tendencies that expressed themselves in a *meaningful* way. The enormous challenge lay in the fact that this infant was a pre-verbal being, or, in the case of very young children, that their linguistic skills and their abstract, reasoning capabilities were not yet fully-developed. Nevertheless, Klein's work addressed this pre-verbal world and showed how it was alive with unconscious fantasies, fantasies which are present from the very beginning of life. For her, these fantasies, formed amidst intersubjective, communicative relations, create the possibility of our verbal, conscious identities of ourselves.

Not surprisingly, Klein's vocabulary sometimes falls short of her colossal task. The baby is not really thinking, 'I am going to bite the breast, because I hate my mother and I wish she was dead because she has all this lovely warm milk which she only gives me a little at a time, and I wish it was all mine.' Klein needed to create a vocabulary, a technique and a way of looking at this previously 'impersonal' baby which would bring to the fore the meaning of its internal world, and she did so. Technique and vocabulary have since evolved, but the emphasis on the unconscious fantasies and on the ways of relating to the object (as opposed to pure instinctual force) remains a central feature of the Kleinian school.

Klein's main strength was her clinical experience with children and her capacity for interpreting their play in terms of unconscious fantasies. This extension of Freud's method of encompassing previously unattended-to phenomena led Kleinians to look for the meaning not just of words, but of play and of the ways in which we relate to others, verbally, non-verbally and even pre-verbally. As mentioned before, this point had extremely rich consequences for psychoanalytical technique, with Kleinians being particularly concerned with what the patient does by saying what he says, and with what he conveys to the analyst by doing so. This led to an awareness of the countertransference, or the feelings evoked in the analyst by virtue of the projections of the patient.

The crucial point here is that the projections and introjections, which are mechanisms of defence and of the constitution of the ego and the superego, are also communicative interactions between the mother and the baby, or the patient and the analyst. Projections are the externalizations of unconscious fantasies and, as such, they achieve a primitive form of communication. In our day-to-day interaction we are sometimes surprised by certain feelings of alarm or urgency conveyed by the perfectly innocuous report of a friend, and this disparity, as well as the intensity of feelings generated, makes us pay more attention to what is being said or, perhaps, to look at what is *not* said. As mothers, we are aware of the real capacity for communication of an otherwise non-verbal, non-'rational' baby. Klein recognizes the relevance of these very primitive fantasies, how enmeshed they are with our ways of being in the world, and how they shape our more mature capacities. Moreover, she is also aware of the rage, violence and aggression provoked by this early situation of dependency, and how these feelings also express themselves and shape our identities as social, rational and mature beings.

Seen in this light, the whole feeding experience gains a new meaning. What is being fed is really the capacity of the child for forming a communicative relationship and for integrating love and hatred. The baby conveys to the mother its needs, both physical and psychic. There is, from the start, a complex world of internal objects that feed and rest contentedly but also devour and attack. The 'good enough mother' provides not just milk and love, but a space where the feelings of hatred and destructiveness can begin to be absorbed and symbolized in a communicative interaction. What is initially projected into the mother with enormous violence can, depending on the development of the interaction, begin to become a more symbolic and linguistically mediated interaction. This, of course, involves the unconscious world of the mother, her own capacity for holding and digesting these raw and sometimes very powerful feelings, and returning them to the baby in a way that will allow it to begin the integration of love and hatred. The possibility of creating links to mediate between separate objects, that is, the possibility of rational thought and symbolization, is, according to Klein and her followers, embedded in an emotional, pre-verbal communicative interaction which is, moreover, an experience of dependency and loss. This inevitably provokes in the omnipotent and narcissistic baby deep feelings of love and hatred, feelings which are not easy to integrate.[135]

This understanding of the role of the conflict between love and hatred in our very early interactions and their mental counterparts led Klein to develop, in her later works, the idea of positions. There are two positions for Klein: the paranoid–schizoid and the depressive positions. A position, as Hinshelwood notes, is a 'constellation of anxieties, defences, object-relations and impulses'.[136] It denotes a certain mental state characterized by specific fantasies and mechanisms of defence.

In the paranoid-schizoid position, the world is roughly divided into good and bad, where the good is idealized in order to protect it from the destructive attacks of the bad object. The internal object has to be split, and the ego uses continuous mechanisms of projections and introjections in a vain attempt to keep off the persecutory retaliatory attacks. This is, by now, a familiar picture, as it follows the very primitive early mechanisms of the incipient ego described earlier. In this mode, the splittings between the good and the bad objects are excessive, leading to an incapability of experiencing the object as a whole. This type of splitting can lead to fragmentation and the creation of what Bion called 'bizarre objects', creating distortions in thinking or non-thinking.

In the case of the depressive position, there is a movement towards an integration of the bad and the good object, in terms of a less idealized good object and a less persecutory bad one which can accept the ambivalences of love and hatred. The capacity for tolerating our own aggression and violence is accompanied by a lessening of our idealization of the good, which makes for a more gentle, less narcissistically demanding superego. The pain of the depressive position is, however, enormous, as one is faced with the unbearable experience of separateness, exclusion and difference, leading to manic defences of omnipotence, denial and denigration. In this case, it might seem as if we are thinking and reflecting when, in fact, we might be using thought in order not to think.

As many commentators have pointed out,[137] Klein was departing from the more classical Freudian theory of libidinal stages of development. Although the paranoid position is the first form of relationship with our objects, and the depressive position a later developmental stage, the first one is never completely overcome, nor is the depressive position a permanent achievement. In fact, the idea of positions is an acknowledgement of the dynamic aspect of the interaction between our internal world of object-relations and the external world of intersubjective relations. It is a recognition of the to-ing and fro-ing of regressions and achievements which colour the ways in which we negotiate new challenges and losses. The Freudian libidinal stages express themselves inside, rather than outside these positions. Moreover, the emphasis on the positions is a departure from classical theory, which also freed Klein to develop Freud's later insights on the death instinct.

Klein's greatest contribution is her development of the death instinct and how it can indeed destroy the goodness of an object. The splittings and further idealizations of the good as a protection against attacks can only intensify those attacks, for the idealized object provokes, she argued, an enormous envy which will lead to further splittings and the fragmentation of the ego. Klein developed the concept of envy to account for a spoiling of the object which is not necessarily related to the frustration of having to wait for the breast. Moreover, envy is different from jealousy, which is related to the Oedipus complex, that is, to the love for one whole person, the mother, and to the wish to remove another, the father. Jealousy of the father leads to the introjection of a father-figure which is both severe and creative, persecutory and potent. With envy, the picture is darker. Indeed, the narcissistic wish to have the object is more destructive of the separateness of the object than the wish to become 'like' it (the Oedipal identification). Moreover, as Segal points out, envy is more than the baby's wish to have the breast all for itself. It can start that way, though the crucial point is that when the baby feels that this task is impossible, its envious attacks are aimed at the destruction of the breast. Envy 'aims at spoiling the goodness of the object, to remove the source of envious feelings.'[138] Envy is the expression of the death instinct, the destructive attack on what is good precisely because it is good and affirmative of life.

This idea of an inborn destructive tendency, allied, no doubt, to the love instinct in so far as it does arise from the narcissistic wish to be and to have the object, has been challenged by various schools of psychoanalysis and more specifically by ego-psychologists. The examples from clinical material can be read in various ways. The negative therapeutic reaction, that is, the difficulty of taking in the interpretation precisely because it is good, can be seen from an ego-psychologist's view as an example of the healthy refusal of an eccentric interpretation based on the questionable idea of a death instinct.[139] This is precisely, however, where Klein has the upper hand over her adversaries, for she recognizes that the unconscious harbours both the deadliness of the instinct as well as its vitality. The mark of the depressive position is our ability to integrate the good and the bad. In the more primitive position we need to keep these two far apart, through splittings and projections. Klein and her followers recognize how the good can become the bad and the bad good, how there are constellations of feelings rather than clear-cut answers. In these murkier waters, an interpretation has to be seen in the wider context of the person's overall mental configuration, which encompasses the here and now of the session but also the previous sessions and the possible confirmation or refutation of the interpretation following subsequent sessions.

There are no clear-cut answers or decontextualized interpretations. Our defences against envy can create a more complex landscape than the Manichean battle between good and evil which we generally assume to be the case, in a simplistic way. Thus, rather than envying the object, we might devalue it, or devalue the self that wants that object. Or we might appear to feel indifferent, or we might project the envy so that *we* feel envied (and persecuted) rather than the other way around. We might also feel that we have completely – therefore master and control – the object desired within ourselves, thus finding it very difficult to recognize the separateness or difference of the object outside ourselves. Or we might blur the boundaries between good and bad, confuse the self and the other, I and Thou, We and They, in order not to experience the pain of envy. Kleinian psychoanalytical literature is a plea for a more detailed description and understanding of psychic phenomena, seen as expressions of *both* loving *and* destructive impulses which are conscious *and* unconscious. Any understanding of a social world which revolves around the construction of categories and identities can only benefit from Klein's hypotheses, for they draw our attention to that which is excluded, to that which we do not accept, but which, nevertheless, still moulds our perception of the world.

Michael Rustin's perceptive use of Kleinian theory for understanding racism[140] illustrates the relevance and richness of these concepts to the social sciences. He shows how racism draws on primitive emotions using mechanisms of projection and group identification, and how, without understanding these emotions, one might, in fact, be legitimizing racism by taking its intellectual claims seriously. Moreover, he is also able to show how one should be careful, when countering racism, not to draw on the same mechanisms of projection and identification (They-the-racists and Us-the-non-racists) as they might reinforce precisely these feelings that give rise to racism whilst seemingly combatting it.

Another example can be seen in Seyla Benhabib's illuminating and perceptive account of the narcissism that pervades social theory.[141] The myth of an autonomous (male) individual as the starting-point or founding-stone of society is a familiar one, as the stories of Robinson Crusoe or Descartes' isolated subject show. Benhabib argues that this myth has this powerful grasp on our imagination precisely because it denies 'the most natural and basic bond of dependence',[142] namely the dependence on the mother. She quotes Hobbes, who considers men 'as if but even now sprung out of the earth, and suddenly, like mushrooms, come to full maturity, without all kind of engagement to each other'.[143] This is a colourful and revealing example of the wish to eradicate the mother. The consequences for ethics are monumental as, Benhabib argues, underneath the wish for justice of the autonomous self of modern social theory, lurks the violent wishes to deny the female upon whom this autonomous (male) self depends.

This is not a problem restricted to male social theorists or psychologists as some feminists have seemed to imply, for the envy, the violence and the aggression that Klein described are not the prerogative of the male. The simplistic idea of substituting penis-envy for the more feminine qualities, epitomized by the creative womb and the nurturing mother, also misses the point of Klein's understanding of the Oedipus complex. According to J. Temperley, the 'Kleinian view is that it is not primarily the limiting power of the father that has to be accepted but the reality of our separateness, our dependence on objects we do not control and of our relation to parents whose independent intercourse has to be acknowledged'.[144] The socialization brought about by the resolution of the Oedipus complex implies the recognition not just of the power of the father or the nurturing capacities of the mother; it is the recognition of our exclusion and therefore of our separateness from a creative parental *couple*. We may build powerful Robinsonades (even feminist ones) in order to avoid facing up to this painful exclusion. It is the acknowledgement of our narcissism, however, which can, in the end, restore our potency and creativity. By realizing that we do not have the idealized powers of our parents, we might allow them and ourselves to have a more human interaction as separate, dependent, fragile, potent and creative individuals.

Another important contribution Klein can make to the social sciences is her understanding of the guilt provoked by the deadly attacks on the good objects, and our ensuing need to repair, in some way, the damage done. She was always fascinated by the need of even very small children to 'put back together' the toys that they had previously attacked. She also remarked how a real reparation, that is, a putting-together that acknowledges the damage done, as opposed to a manic reparation which acts as if there had been no attack – can bring about a relief from guilt and anxiety that reinforces the affirmative, loving capacities of the child.[145] In fact, the same happens with the feeding of a baby. The appearance of the mother after a particularly angry bout of screaming can diminish the infant's omnipotent belief in its own destructive powers, that is, if the baby can stop screaming for a while and acknowledge in spite of its anger that the breast is there. The good feeding experience that ensues affirms the independence of the breast and reveals, by the same token, the failure of the child's omnipotence. As these good experiences are repeated, the child starts to cope with its feelings of despair and loss by establishing a more durable internal good object. This also brings about a relief from guilt and anxiety, and the child becomes able to experience gratitude.

What had started as a wish to control and possess the object can become, given a bit of luck and the right circumstances, an experience of gratitude for the object's separateness and a wish to care for what is fragile and dependent in ourselves and others. Klein's understanding of love, like Freud's understanding of Eros, changed through the confrontation with the death instinct. F. Alford[146] remarks that Klein's understanding of love is close to the idea of *caritas*. This type of love goes beyond self-interest or the satisfaction of libidinal instincts; it is genuine concern for the other as an 'other', separate and different from me. This capacity for love recognizes the bonds of mutual dependency that make our lives possible, and seeks to restore and repair the damage done to the object by our destructive, narcissistic impulses. The possibility of happiness lies in its capacity for recognizing these bonds, which are not, as Habermas claims, symmetrical relations between equal subjects, but relations of dependency between unequal ones. Our caring and concern for the internal objects and external subjects are what create the possibility for happiness in the internal and the external social worlds.

If Klein is right, Thanatos and Eros are there from the beginning. Morality, in this sense, is not a pact between autonomous, mature beings, nor does it start with the resolution of the Oedipus complex. In fact, for Klein, the Oedipus conflict happens at a much earlier stage than for Freud. In her account, we are struggling with our aggression and our love from the very beginning. We are therefore deeply moral beings from the start, for the restoration of good internal objects is a fundamental condition of our happiness, not to say our sanity. The internal and social worlds are intrinsically linked and prone to the same destructive, aggressive, narcissistic attacks. Alford makes the interesting point that the two basic positions of Melanie Klein's theory can be linked to two different conceptions of morality. In the more primitive 'talion' morality (an eye for an eye), every act of aggression (fantasized or not) is returned in kind, a way of thinking and interacting characteristic of the paranoid–schizoid position. In the depressive position, the individual is more capable of identifying with the other person's pain, leading in some way to what Alford calls a 'reparative' morality. This is close to the modernist's concern, in social theory, with imagining and desiring a world where justice could be done to all. Interestingly enough, Klein distinguishes between a 'real' reparation in the depressive position and the manic reparation which is still within the paranoid–schizoid position. In this latter case, although there is a frantic wish to make things right, there is no acknowledgement of the damage we have done. H. Segal[147] argues that in this type of reparation, we distance ourselves from the original object. Then we can direct the reparative wishes to a distant, less meaningful object, or to objects to which we feel superior. The bizarreness of the Hobbesian picture of men as mushrooms, or the detachment of the veil of ignorance proposed by Rawls' theory of justice, which we shall discuss in the following chapter, are telling signs of a distance that must be created between ourselves and others. From this detached, superior position, we might even try to be fair and just to those who are not like ourselves ('poor things!'). This regal gesture, however, will never succeed in bringing about the relief from guilt that a true reparation and concern for the other does. The depressive position is not the manic wish to create a world of justice where no evil can rule; it is the acknowledgement of our envious attacks on what is most important in ourselves and in others: our mutual dependency.

Klein is famous for having given the death instinct a prominent, centre-stage position. Her real achievement, however, is her understanding of love as reparation (*caritas*), intrinsically linked to the reality of the death instinct. Thus, it is not the death instinct but the battle between life and death that takes centre-stage. It is not envy but envy *and* gratitude, Eros *and* Thanatos that concern Klein. Love as the concern for an object other than ourselves only gains its meaning when approached against the background of the power of our destructive instincts. From this recognition come our more mature capacities for thought and reflection. Thus, the responsibility for the other is not just a duty to the other person, but a basic precondition of our own happiness.

One could still argue, and this is generally the argument against Klein, that to see everything in terms of an 'internal' world of objects is to reduce the richness of the social world to the purely psychological. This is missing the point of Klein's contribution. There is no purely 'internal', psychological battle. The categories of internal and external are formed by our perceptions of an intersubjective, interhuman world, where emotion and cognition, conscious and unconscious thoughts and affects are not separate, distinct entities. Klein enables us to think of these interrelations, showing how personal happiness is indissociable from social responsibility. To understand the idea of *caritas*, however, the concern for the other as moral happiness, one also has to accept the inevitable destructiveness of the death instinct. The 'other' of reason is not the idealized libidinal desire, nor that which has not yet been thought but which, once thought, will become the same as what was already known. The unconscious, for Kleinians, is both life and death, both affirmation and negation of life. Thinking about it is creating a space for what has not yet been thought. This is where Habermas and Lyotard, modern and postmodern traditions alike, fall short of the task.

5

THE MOVE TO ETHICS: HABERMAS

The central problem for moral philosophy is the question of judgement, which, of course, involves the problem of the norms and the criteria used for its justification. The hermeneutic-inspired philosophy has always argued that these norms must be judged on the basis of the values that a community shares. For the hermeneutic tradition, which, as we have already mentioned, has influenced our postmodern distrust of universalist theories, there is no vantage point outside a shared world of meanings, as outside such a world there is no possibility of communication. We are always already within language, and therefore we are always full of prejudices, that is, of pre-judgements, values and ideas that are part of our capacity for judging rather than hindrances to it. The fact that we belong to a world of shared values is what makes us capable of delivering judgements. Indeed, because we belong to a group or a community, we also share its idea of the good, and can therefore decide on the evilness of, say, an action by a group or an individual, or the appropriateness of a law for the community. Without this rich world of values which shapes and forms our judgements, we would be incapable of moral choices.

The move from epistemology to language helped to establish this approach as the culturally sensitive one. Indeed, Peter Winch's paper 'Understanding a Primitive Culture'[148] was a landmark that aimed to show how our scientifically-oriented culture could, in fact, destroy rather than produce knowledge. He claimed that Evans-Pritchard's use of scientific categories, as if they were neutral standards of judgement, distorted his understanding of the Azande. According to Winch, openly indebted to Wittgenstein, we necessarily approach other cultures with the values and prejudices that belong to our own forms of life (as in the case of Evans-Pritchard and his idea of science as a neutral form of knowledge). We should not seek to deny this, as without this background which forms our language games, we could not communicate. The search for a standpoint outside of language, even if this standpoint is deemed 'scientific', is futile. For Winch, the way forward is to acknowledge this background and to engage in a conversation with the different cultural conceptions. His idea is to use our background to understand the other's point of view, instead of distancing ourselves from what is unknown as inferior to our own cultural achievements. Instead of using scientific categories to label as primitive the Aboriginal practice of carrying about a stick as if it embodied the soul, we would do better to remind ourselves of the way lovers in our culture have carried about a picture or a lock of hair of their beloved and of how distraught they can be when losing that hair or that picture. This is not only in order to make the Aboriginal practice less incomprehensible, infantile or primitive by our standards; it is also a means of suggesting a fresh look at our own conceptions and rituals of love, life and death, now enriched by our capacities for understanding other ways of going about the world. With the linguistic turn, the search for truth, which in the epistemological framework was epitomized by the scientific experiment in a controlled environment, became the metaphor of conversation and dialogue. The moment of truth became the opening up of different backgrounds, with a transformation of both ourselves and the 'other' in the process, what Gadamer called a fusion of horizons.[149]

The problem with this view, however, is that once we emphasize the different possible interpretations of the meanings of our language practices, there is no way we can justify one interpretation over another. In a sense, by multiplying the possible forms of life, we make the ideas of truth, justice and rightness weaker and harder to defend, as they can be shown to mean different things to different people at different times. One of the possible answers to this conundrum is to refer the interpretations to the overall life of a community and to show that even though the multiplication of views is a possibility, there is still a consistency and a continuity in the overall life of a community that an interpretation must follow.[150]

This is not the end of the problem. A truly hermeneutic understanding has also shown us that even what we understand to be the accepted standards and values of a community is an interpretation of an interpretation (what is taken to be the community's understanding of itself), and that there is no way of getting to the 'bottom', or to the 'reality' of this. We are linguistic beings caught in a hermeneutic circle, which has no beginning and no outside point. As Derrida famously remarked, 'Il n'y a pas de hors-texte': there is no outside the text. And even if we were to agree on a framework as being that of the minimal, culturally-shared values of a community, which, as we just said, will itself be problematic or at least open to new interpretations, we would still run into problems. Indeed, practically no one would regard the Holocaust as justifiable on the basis of its conformity to and consistency with the values of Nazism. The tolerance previously glimpsed through the idea of conversations and dialogue, can become a dangerous lack of a critical view. Thus, we are left, at best, with a meaningless gesture and, at worst, with a possible conformity to the dominant view. By dominant view, it is not necessary to understand solely the usual culprits, that is, Western capitalist societies. In our attempts to be politically correct in our multicultural societies, it is quite easy to feel the weight of having to follow some given group's views for fear of imposing our own – generally assumed to be Western, white, male, Christian views, even when we are non-white, female, non-Christian and third world. The terrorism of the multiplicity of views can destroy the very idea of respect for difference, by reducing the idea of critique to a Western, capitalist privilege. Without it, however, we just conform.

The idea of critique, central to the project of modernity, comes from the Enlightenment tradition. It is inspired by Kantian philosophy and seeks to find in reason and in reason alone the idea of justice and the morally right. This approach promotes an idea of reason as independent of particular interests, values and conceptions of the good. Therefore, rather than seeking to justify a particular rational choice on the basis of the values and aims of a certain community, it seeks to justify it in terms of its universal character. In other words, what makes a moral choice valid is its universality, guaranteed by the use of formal rational procedures. The aim here is precisely to step out of any particular conceptions of the good, which might be tainted by the vested or open interests of an individual, a group or a community, and to move to an idea of justice as independent of any particular circumstances. The Kantian Categorical Imperative is the demand to ground moral norms in a universal idea rather than in individual need. Reason, in the Kantian tradition which inspires the idea of a critical theory upheld by Habermas, is the source of the demand to overcome the distortions inflicted upon our choices by the specific interests or needs of particular groups or individuals in a community.

The danger with this point of view is that it can be shown to be too formal and detached from the particular conceptions of the good in a community to be of relevance to the real moral life of specific members of this community. This, as we know, is the critique of Kant by Hegel. For Hegel, Kant's ethics were too formal; in so far as the agent has to abstract from the concrete content of duties and maxims, they become empty. Moreover, according to Hegel, the universalism to which Kant aspired makes a judgement too abstract, thus making it irrelevant to particular cases. The distance thus created between the realm of real life (what 'is') and morality (what 'ought to be') becomes an unbreachable distance between theory and practice. This can lead to what Habermas calls a 'terrorism' of pure conviction, in so far as the Categorical Imperative '... necessarily recommends to the advocates of the moral world view a policy that aims at the actualization of reason and sanctions even immoral deeds if they serve higher ends'.[151] Hegel's example in the section 'Virtue and the Way of the World' in the *The Phenomenology of Spirit* was the Jacobin zeal to implement their idea of the moral and how it led to the destruction of individuals and individuality. As Lyotard reminds us time and again,[152] the crimes committed in the name of the proletariat or freedom are too big and too recent for us to forget or dismiss.

One of the best known contemporary attempts to ground the ideas of justice in a rational theory is Rawls' *A Theory of Justice*. Still, Rawls' wish to find the rational principles that could ground an idea of justice shared by all, springs from his recognition of the unavoidable diversity of conceptions of the good. He proposed an 'original position' in which agents are to choose the principles of justice behind a 'veil of ignorance' of what is to be their particular situation in society.[153] This is meant to guarantee a view of justice as fairness, as no specific advantages can be sought by the parties so long as they remain unaware of which particular interests should be furthered. If I can be either a very privileged or an extremely exploited person in a particular community, and if I am to choose the principles of justice that should guide this community, I would have to seek the ones that would benefit or, at least, be least harmful to all parties. Rawls reminds us, however, that this original position is a hypothetical situation, not an original state of nature nor a more primitive state of societies, as the old defenders of social contract theory would have had us believe. Indeed, for Rawls, and this has become even clearer in his more recent work, the original position is closer to a device of representation that illustrates what *we regard* as equality and freedom. Still, the recognition of the culturally dependent meaning of our institutions and intuitions does not stop Rawls looking for a rational agreement between the parties. The original position is also a device through which an agreement can be reached via a reflective equilibrium between reasonable shared conceptions of justice and rational principles.[154]

As can be seen in the case of Rawls, there is no doubt that the linguistic turn has made the idea of critique itself a hermeneutic one, in the sense that the philosophers of modernity now accept that universality is an ideal striven for from within language. In fact, they recognize themselves as belonging to a tradition, with its own background of prejudices and ideas. This recognition, however, cannot invalidate the striving for a critical point of view. Unlike the uncritical idea of Dialectical Materialism,[155] Habermas's approach acknowledges that critique is part of the crisis it is supposed to understand. This recognition, which is a fundamental insight into the project of modernity, does not prevent such philosophers from pursuing the idea of critique. Indeed, one can understand Habermas, as Richard Bernstein has done,[156] by remembering that he is a thinker who grew up in Nazi Germany, and that his paramount wish remains therefore to avoid the mistakes and horrors of the past, mistakes that include theories that sought to excuse and justify such horrors. The same understanding applies to Richard Rorty, as belonging to an American Pragmatist tradition that has never experienced the actual horror of defeat or collaboration under the Nazis. But referring a thinker back to his circumstances does not, as Habermas points out in the case of Heidegger, fully explain, let alone excuse, his limitations or contributions. Indeed, in the light of our contemporary fondness for biographies and explanations in terms of personal 'small' histories, this type of explanation is itself open to the same reading. Once again, we find ourselves without means of judging or justifying this interpretation, as it is nothing more than one possible interpretation amongst others. Habermas once famously argued that he must be on the right course as conservative forces in Germany were attacking his idea of critique.[157] Richard Rorty, the American champion of postmodernism, also derived the same satisfaction from knowing that *his* critique of universalism attacked the bastions of Reaganite conservatism, with their defence of a particular position as representing a universal moral truth.[158] This is not an argument in favour of the postmodern, however, rather the opposite, for, if tables can be turned around so easily, we are more than ever in need of showing how to evaluate and distinguish between two readings or two interpretations.

Indeed, Habermas has argued that the defence of pluralism and the recognition of the multiplicity of different cultural backgrounds actually requires a general theory of justice and a moral point of view that could adjudicate between competing moral claims. For him, a world which respects differences is a world that searches for justice and fairness. He has pointed out many times how the shift to postmodernism, cultural relativism and historicism is generally followed by a neo-conservatism which bases the now elusive idea of truth either on a mystical being or on nature. In this case, the recognition of the role of culture can ultimately undermine itself. As Habermas puts it, '[for the neo-conservatives] the universal features of human culture owe their existence more to human nature than to the rational infrastructure of human language, cognition and action, that is, to culture itself.'[159] As we have argued before with the example of Derek Freeman, the recognition of the interpretive dimension of human life can produce a disenchantment that resuscitates a form of naturalism which is intrinsically conservative. The recognition that language is a tool that can be used also to deceive, can lead us to forget that deception is a move that we can make only in language, in so far as language presupposes an idea of understanding and communication that is deliberately overturned. Language provides the capacity for fooling, because it is also, and fundamentally so, a capacity for communication and, therefore, for arguing and for adjudication between disagreements. The dazzle of relativism led Freeman to resort, as many neo-conservatives do, to a belief that truth is to be found in nature, in his case in the physical presentation of one of Margaret Mead's informants (regardless of her own self-acknowledgement as a liar) in front of the 'objectivity' of the camera.[160] The present disenchantment with the social and human sciences, given their degrees of uncertainty and relativism, has produced a revival of research into the genetic features of human nature that are supposed to define our scope for action. Not surprisingly, a belief in racially and genetically defined IQs, as the authors of *The Bell Curve*[161] have proposed, has captured the popular imagination. In our modern efficient world, demanding quick results and palpable evidence, psychoanalysis – or indeed any interpretive social science which upholds an idea of truth and insight to be reached through language and dialogue – does not have much chance when compared to the 'hard evidence' of numbers and genetically determined realities.

The great achievement of Habermas has been his capacity for showing how our options are not reduced to one between abstract and formal universalism on one hand, and meaningless and neo-conservative relativism on the other. For him, the linguistic turn opens a hermeneutic dimension that can lead to the postmodern fragmentation of any universal ideas of truth and justice, but it can also, as we have already shown, bring to the fore the intersubjectivity of human communication, which could become the rational ground for a new ethics. Indeed, if in the epistemological mode we were observers of objects from which we had stood at a distance, our taking the linguistic turn meant that we rediscovered ourselves as participants in a communicative interaction. As participants in communication, we faced the vertigo of reflexivity that gave rise to our postmodern mood. But, by the same token, we also became aware of a type of knowledge or competence that all of us, as participants in communication, must possess. Indeed, for Habermas, this knowledge, which reveals the fact of our belonging to a social world, is what makes any understanding of ourselves as separate, autonomous beings possible. The mistake of most rational ethical projects lies in their attempts to start from an isolated subject and then to proceed to generalize all other subjects. Although such attempts, in so far as they try to produce a universal theory of justice based on reason, attract Habermas's sympathy, they are, from his point of view, bound to fail.

To take the already mentioned case of Rawls, it is difficult to understand what subjects, deprived of their specific positions, values and personalities behind a veil of ignorance, could choose, given that they have been deprived of the rich lifeworld that gives substance to their choices. We could therefore also question the relevance that those choices could have for the community to which the subjects belonged. As Dworkin has pointed out,[162] it is difficult to conceive why an individual would consent to the original position in the first place. Moreover, it is also questionable to assume that, once out from behind the veil of ignorance, individuals would abide by the choices they had made there. The idea of starting from the isolated subject is a remnant of the epistemological framework that owes so much to Descartes. This framework was used with great success in the empirical sciences, but the attempt to use it with moral phenomena actually makes it impossible for the observer to experience the very phenomena he would want to understand, namely moral phenomena as intersubjective phenomena. It is by being practically engaged in everyday life that we experience moral feelings and that problems of justification of our actions as right or wrong arise. In order to experience this, we have to be part of this intersubjective world, not as observers trying to generalize our experience but as partners in a communicative interaction. In fact, Habermas will go one step further. He will claim that it is this very engagement in the intersubjective practical domain that gives us the conditions of possibility of judgement. Indeed, as partners in communication, we all possess an implicit know-how that enables us to interact meaningfully, a know-how that Habermas has called a communicative competence. This competence involves the mutual expectation that we should account for the validity claims of truth, rightness and sincerity that we raise in language. In other words, communication has a rational validity basis in terms of the inbuilt expectations that claims should be explained or justified. This competence for Habermas is not concerned with the specific content that such justification could have, as this relates to what counts as 'good' reasons in a specific situationath; rer, the important feature that Habermas's theory of communicative competence underlines is the rational dimension of communication as relying on an expectation that it is possible, indeed necessary, to maintain the idea that we could, ideally, decide what counts as true or right by use of rational argument alone. From this understanding of communication, Habermas derives the idea that there are rational principles of the moral and practical domain that transcend the specificities of particular ethical values (*Sittlichkeit*), whilst acknowledging the rich lifeworld that gives substance to any idea of justice, (in so far as it is language itself as a communicative practice that reveals these rational principles).

As we saw earlier,[163] the three validity claims of truth, rightness and truthfulness reveal three different worlds referred to by speech acts, namely 'the objective world (as the totality of existing states of affairs), ... the shared social world (as the totality of the legitimately regulated interpersonal relationships of a social group), ...and the subjective world (as the totality of experiences to which one has private access)'.[164] In the case of communicative action, speakers seek to motivate the other rationally to accept such claims not by virtue of the intrinsic validity of what has been said, but by the fact that there is a mutual presumption that, if need be, they can provide reasons for them. In the case of truthfulness or sincerity, the reasons are expected to be demonstrated by future courses of action and behaviour. In the case of truth and rightness, the offer implies an expectation of engaging in a situation of argumentation that Habermas calls discourse, that is, a process of communication with the goal of reaching a *rationally motivated agreement*. This idea, implicit in language, is the ideal speech situation, an idea that is still maintained by Habermas but now more carefully worded, in view of the fact that it is so easy to misuse it. Discourse is a process of argumentation which involves the refusal of external or internal coercion; it assumes that an agreement can be reached in conditions of symmetry and equality, where only the force of reason prevails.[165]

With this approach, Habermas is making two fundamental points. The first is that the moral domain is open to knowledge and evaluation and therefore calls for rational justification, though Habermas is careful to point out that this justification is on a different level from the justification of truth. Habermas's moral cognitivism distinguishes between the rightness of the moral domain and the truth of the world of empirical states of affairs.[166] He draws on Strawson's essay 'Freedom and Resentment'[167] to show not only that there are reasons for our moral conduct that must be open to rational argumentation, but also that without this understanding, the specificity of the moral domain as belonging to an intersubjective world of shared norms and obligations loses its meaning. Habermas also mentions in this respect Durkheim's understanding of the suprapersonal world of norms as involving a moral authority that cannot be reduced merely to the power and fear of sanctions, but has also to rely on reasons for compliance.[168] Indeed, the ability to understand moral phenomena *qua* moral phenomena relies on our capacity for seeing this suprapersonal world of bonding and binding obligations as a world of shared norms, which has to rely on reasons for its existence. Applied to mass societies, this means that there is no mass loyalty without legitimacy. As Habermas argues, '... if in the long run the social currency of a norm depends on its being accepted as valid in the group to which it is addressed and if this recognition is based in turn in the expectation that the corresponding claim to validity can be redeemed with reasons, it follows that there is a connection between the "existence" of a norm and the anticipated justifiability of the corresponding "ought" statement, a connection for which there is no parallel in the ontic sphere'.[169]

The second point stems from this recognition that the moral world is inextricably bound to the reasons we give for our actions in discourse. This recognition has definitely departed from the old epistemological framework of an isolated subjectivity, and the moral cognitivism proposed cannot be reduced to the old project and its ideas of truth and science. The most important point, however, is that this new proposal allows Habermas to redevelop the idea of a universalist moral theory, so central to the modernity project, in terms of the pragmatics of communication.

The use of the principle of universalization in moral theory is central to the tradition of modernity. In spite of what postmodern philosophers generally say,[170] the philosophers of modernity acknowledge the diversity of competing forms of life, but, precisely because they are suspicious of the power of force or ignorance to impose one view to the detriment of others, they seek to find, in reason alone, a moral principle that would respect the 'other' as a free and equal person. In other words, moral norms have to pass the test of generalization and universalization in order to be acceptable as truly *moral* norms. The moral dimension forces the recognition of the 'other' as an autonomous subject, equal to oneself. The same idea of autonomy and freedom is present in Freud, in his idea that freedom can be found only in a recognition of reality, or, to put it differently, that autonomous subjects must recognize and distinguish between the world of their unconscious and primitive wishes and the reality of the world we all interact with, which, of course, is the world of other subjects, who are as entitled to happiness and freedom as ourselves.

The difficulties of this project were to be found mainly in the justification of the principle of universalization. Indeed, if we start from the isolated subject, fending for him or herself, it is impossible actually to link this 'island' with the radically different 'other'. Accepting the rule of universalization could then be seen as an attempt to impose our own (culturally dependent, etc.) views upon others. Rather than a project of emancipation, the acceptance of such a rule could lead to the imposition of 'our' Western types of rationalization onto other worlds. The acceptance of Freud's views only adds a further twist to this difficult realization, in so far as we must accept that, whilst on the surface working in a rational universalizing direction, we might be fulfilling unconscious impulses that could actually destroy the more conscious wishes for respect and recognition of others.

The great contribution of Habermas to this discussion is his reworking of the principle of universalization (U)[171] in terms of the transcendental pragmatic conditions of communication. He has argued that we start from a situation of intersubjectivity, and that it is only within this intersubjectivity that moral phenomena and moral problems arise. Moreover, this situation of intersubjectivity implies certain unavoidable presuppositions of communication,[172] namely that in order to communicate we share an ideal of an agreement between equal partners to be striven for in discourse. Habermas therefore reformulates the universalization principle in terms of the argumentation to be pursued by partners in discourse. Moral norms demand the recognition by all those concerned in so far as they aspire to be moral norms, but this recognition has to be produced in a situation of communication by partners seeking an agreement. This is no longer the universalization of an isolated subject seeking to prescribe to all and on behalf of all; it is now a discursive test amongst partners in communication of what *could be agreed by all to be a universal norm.*[173]

In order to justify this position, Habermas relies on his own theory of communicative action and on K.-O. Apel's transcendental pragmatic analyses,[174] more specifically on Apel's argument of a 'performative contradiction'.[175] This idea implies that whoever doubts or questions that such transcendental presuppositions are necessary for communication is in effect using them to articulate and express his own doubt. In order to argue that there are no rules that are irreplaceable in argumentation, one is, in fact, entering into argumentation and therefore assuming that what is being said can be understood as an argument against argumentation. As Habermas puts it, 'Every argumentation, regardless of the context in which it occurs, rests on pragmatic presuppositions from whose propositional content the principle of universalism (U) can be derived'.[176] This is, of course, far from the old dream of an ultimate foundation for discourse. What Habermas is claiming does not take one outside or beyond language; if anything, his argument places us squarely back within language. Still, the formal pragmatic features of language reveal the presence of a universalizing principle, and this principle forms the basis of a discourse ethics.[177] By discourse ethics, Habermas means an ethics that aims at universal norms, to be tested and grounded in the concrete argumentation between equal partners attempting to uphold the universalistic principles that guide our ideas of discourse. This universalizing principle, however, is forever present in actual specific historical and situational argumentations, as these take place amongst real partners in discourse. The modernity ideal of universal rational principles can only be upheld once we acknowledge the intersubjective dimension of rationality. An ethics of autonomy must necessarily be an ethics of solidarity. Once we recognize that language provides the rational principles for discourse as well as the concrete possibility of argumentation between partners, the ideal of autonomy becomes inextricably bound to the bonds of solidarity, with the duty to achieve, in discourse, the very ideals of respect, fairness and equality promised in language.

There is another route to a possible justification of this principle of universalization, and this is via Melanie Klein's development and reworking of Freud's psychoanalytical theory in terms of the object-relations, established from the onset of life,[178] between subjects. It is important to repeat once again that the term object-relations theory emphasizes the relational dimension of the mental world by concentrating on the object of the instinct (the breast, the penis, the mother, the father), rather than on the energetical balance or on the body that produces the instinct. This idea by no means implies that we relate mainly to a world of objects of nature, nor that we objectify the subjects we relate to. Some psychoanalysts have even argued for a possible change of terminology (a 'subject-relations theory'), a change that might have the advantage of clarifying the emphasis placed by this approach on our intersubjectivity. The problem with calling it a 'subject-relations theory' is that it could imply the idea of whole subjects relating to each other, and this is also misleading, for what is being examined is the link between different, sometimes conflicting aspects of subjects and how the relationships thus established help to create our identities as subjects.

Klein and her followers have stressed how these different aspects of ourselves could relate differently, not only to others but also to each other, and this may sometimes leave us with a very confused picture of where 'we' (if there is any such determinate reference group) stand. This is made clear by the tentative jargon used in psychoanalytical sessions, in terms of how a 'part of the patient' feels this, whereas 'another part of the patient' might feel just the opposite. We are, of course, not divided into small pieces nor can we distinguish so clearly between parts of ourselves. One of Klein's points is that such a sharp divide between these 'parts' and the inability to tolerate ambivalence reveals that we are functioning within the confines of the paranoid position, with its mechanisms of splitting and projection. These mechanisms can endanger our identities and capacities for happiness, associated, in Klein's terminology, with the depressive position. The defence mechanisms place 'outside ourselves' the feelings or thoughts that we cannot contain or accept, and we project onto others (who thereby become bad, unthoughtful, critical, etc.) what we cannot accept within ourselves. This process, as we have already mentioned, leads to fear and persecution as we are now open to the *internal* retaliatory attacks of these 'bad' objects (the Jew, the Arab, the Black, our next-door neighbour, our rival at work, or in the case of psychotic modes of functioning, concrete and bizarre objects that have gained specific meanings). These objects become even more powerful thanks to our added projections.

This process, of course, is not simply an interaction between an outer and an inner world. Indeed, this world of fantasies is our own, but it reveals the world of relationships to others. We bear, within ourselves, as 'internal objects', these ways of relating to the world in terms of idealized or damaged and persecutory objects, and these ways delimit and determine our capacity for perceiving new objects and situations. The very important point is that Klein does not draw a line between the external and the internal worlds, nor does she, as many adversaries have it, stress the internal to the detriment of the external world. By stressing the links between objects, Klein is able to show meticulously how, in relating to others, we construct representations of objects that determine what we consider 'outside' and 'inside'. This 'internal' world colours both our understanding of ourselves and others, but this internal world is a mental representation of an *intersubjective* world.

Not surprisingly, Klein and her followers have been accused of betraying Freud and creating a psychoanalytical ethics instead of a scientific theory of sexuality (as instinctual energy). The question here is not so much whether psychoanalysis, as any practice, contains and disseminates a particular *Weltanschauung*, a suggestion that Freud was particularly keen to refute, on the grounds of the scientificity and therefore the impartiality of psychoanalysis.[179] As Figueira pointed out, psychoanalysis disseminates ideas and is itself a 'culture' and a worldview. Indeed, there is no doubt that Freud and psychoanalysis in general share some of the ideals of the Enlightenment, most particularly the ideal of autonomy and maturity (*Mundigkeit*) as a basis for personal happiness. What is being said here, however, is slightly different. It has been said that Kleinians have moved away from Freud's theory of sexuality by privileging the moral dimension of the struggle between our aggression and our need to repair the damage done. This is indeed correct, but this might be the strength rather than the weakness of Klein's views. By emphasizing how we rely on our (very early) relationships to others to create a sense of ourselves, and by examining the ways through which we try to avoid responsibility for our actions and feelings (for instance, by projecting our feelings onto others), Klein departed from the remnants of a more naturalistic approach to analysis, which saw it as a process of almost solitary remembering. The popular myth of a silent analyst mumbling an assent to the patient's uninterrupted flow of reminiscences is not common within the Kleinian school, where the analyst engages immediately in the interpretative process of the interaction within the analytical setting. Moreover, the image of analysis as recovering a forgotten truth is also shattered. Instead of promising happiness as the outcome of the psychoanalytical process, Klein stresses the imperative need to reintegrate in the here and now the responsibilities for the attacks we do and have done to our objects as a first step towards a meaningful reparation, which is an expression of love and a precondition of happiness.

In the depressive position, we are more able to recognize and reintegrate the parts of ourselves that were pushed onto others and to feel the guilt for the damage we might have done. In so doing, we are redrawing the boundaries between ourselves and others, and slowly accepting the existence of others and of the relations between others. This work, however, is not done once and for all, and we are always vulnerable to a shift back to the mechanisms of the paranoid position, with its splittings and fragmentation of our emotional world and of our capacity for thinking.

What psychoanalytical clinical literature has shown is that the understanding of ourselves and others as containing both good and bad, and as inextricably linked to others by bonds that create both love and hate, consolidates the depressive position and allows for the possibility of thinking, freedom and happiness. The resort to the sharp divide between what is good and what is bad, where the threatening feelings have to be split off and spat out, becomes less frequent and less powerful. For Klein, the autonomy and freedom of a subject are inextricably bound to the recognition of the links that bind him or her to others and to the links between others that might exclude us. The depressive position provides an alternative justification for Habermas's ethics of autonomy as an ethics of solidarity. It also shows, however, the limits of Habermas's discourse theory, as the idea of a transparent dialogue of partners in communication has to be rethought. The recognition of intersubjective bonds does not mean, for Klein, a presumption of equality between participants. In fact, it is quite the opposite, as she recognizes the violent emotions aroused by the inequalities and differences, and explains how we might create imaginary worlds in order to eradicate these differences.

Klein's approach can also work on the resolution of another central problem of Habermas's discourse ethics. Habermas claims that his universalism does not fall into Kant's abstract formalism. The universalist principles that guide discourse ethics, namely the ideas of equality and freedom, are to be redeemed in the concrete situations of actual argumentation. These principles, however, are too broad to be really meaningful for political and moral judgement. As G. Warnke has remarked, 'From the idea that only those norms are valid which could meet with the assent of all those concerned as free and equal participants in a practical discourse, we, as moral theorists, can derive no actual specific norms.'[180] Habermas would answer this criticism by stressing that his project shows the rational dimension of any moral discussion. As communicative rationality, this approach demands that the specific contents and the actual practice of reaching agreement be left outside discourse ethics, as the concrete process of argumentation in a social context, in a particular cultural space and historical time. The criticism remains, however, that the principles of discourse ethics are either too broad or too strict for a substantial contribution to the actual discussion of moral questions. This criticism can be extended to Habermas's political positions. Whitebook, for instance, warns us that 'the call for "constitutional patriotism" based on "abstract procedures and principles" is in danger of remaining "a mere moral ought" in Hegel's sense'.[181]

The contributions of S. Benhabib, a partisan of the project of modernity, have shown a possible direction that a universalist moral theory might take. Her point is that the idea of equality amongst partners in communication might not be sufficient to ensure the ideals of justice and freedom, in so far as they might still exclude from discourse ethics a domain which is fundamental to the idea of justice. Using the feminist critique of Kohlberg's moral stages theory,[182] so central to Habermas's own ideas, Benhabib shows how it furthers a dichotomy between the idea of justice, to be covered by an ethics of equality and fairness, and the idea of the 'good life', restricted to the domain of lived experiences, values and care.[183] By showing how these two domains have generally come to represent the distinction between the public and the private, and how these in turn have come to represent the masculine and the feminine worlds, Benhabib has shown how one can then view the personal and the feminine as *outside* the world of justice, rational discussion and reflection. It is not only the feminine that loses out; the very project of a universalist moral theory becomes endangered. By retrieving what she calls the 'concrete other', Benhabib seeks to show the limitations of a universalist perspective that 'generalizes' the 'other'. Unless we include in the moral domain the questions of 'kinship, love, friendship and sex' that Kohlberg and traditional moral theory want to view as 'personal decision-making', we will keep on privileging a type of question that defines a male-oriented idea of justice. This idea promotes an idea of equality which is fundamentally unequal, and generalizes an 'other' who remains the same: a narcissistic copy of oneself. An ethics of care, with its recognition of the other as an individual with a specific history and feelings, provides a counterbalance to an ethics of justice, with its emphasis on what unites us all as the same, that is, as human beings. Unless we recognize the diversity and the individuality of others, the very project of a universalist moral and political theory that defends rights and duties remains endangered. The recognition that the 'generalized other' is also a 'concrete other' can help redefine a universalism which will no longer be 'an ideal consensus of fictitiously defined selves, but the concrete process in politics and morals of the struggle of concrete, embodied selves, striving for autonomy'.

Melanie Klein's theory stresses the bonds and links that create ourselves as ourselves and others 'as others'. She and her followers have been able to show how our understanding of the 'other' might indeed be a total negation of the 'other's' individuality or capacities. She has shown how the use of projections and introjections makes us place into others what we cannot accept in ourselves, and also, how we can relate to an enviable quality of the other person, which, indeed, we might lack in ourselves, by identifying and incorporating it as our own. In both cases, the individuality and the recognition of the difference and separateness of the other person is effectively denied, and mechanisms of defence stop us from recognizing that we are denying the 'otherness' of the 'other'. For Klein and her followers, the depressive position involves more than the recognition that we belong to a world of others to whom we are inextricably tied. It involves also the recognition of our duties and responsibilities towards this world, in so far as our attacks on others and our mechanisms of defence can actually destroy the individuality and difference of the 'other'. What psychoanalytical literature has shown is that these attacks can be directed not just at the 'other' as another person, but at the bonds of dependence between subjects.

Moreover, these attacks can actually endanger our capacity for thinking, for, as Bion has argued,[184] the capacity for thinking is inextricably tied to the links that the infant is able to establish with its early objects. It is not only that the child needs to introject an object capable of making links, of 'digesting'. Contemporary Kleinians have shown that the child needs to come to terms with and introject a creative 'couple' as a fundamental condition of its thinking capacity. Thus, the destruction or the attacks can be directed at our objects, or, even more seriously, they can affect our very capacity for forming links, for thinking. This is quite clear in Klein's and her followers' understanding of the Oedipus complex.[185]

Klein emphasized the early onset of a primitive Oedipus complex, and how the ways we choose to relate to our most primitive objects (the breast) shape the later resolution of the Oedipus complex. In a sense, she was saying that the way we cope with our hatred and envy are what determine how we negotiate our love and sexual desire at the later time of the Oedipus complex. This approach is very helpful in terms of rethinking Freud's approach to the Oedipus complex and his difficulties in understanding female sexuality.[186] For Klein, the way we deal with (or attack) the separateness and 'otherness' of our objects is what determines our more mature relations to others.[187]

Contemporary Kleinians have stressed that the resolution of the Oedipus complex implies a capacity for recognizing the relationship of the parental couple, a relationship that excludes the child. Thus, the attacks of the child are not just directed at the other parent as a potential rival but at the idea of a couple which exists independently of the child. Britton[188] has used the illuminating image of a triangle, with the child, the father and the mother at each vertex. From there, one can see that the child relates to the mother or the father, but that the mother also relates to the father, in a relationship that excludes the child and creates the triangle as a space. If the link between the parents is impossible for the child to tolerate, then the child cannot introject a 'third position' as 'a space outside the self capable of being observed and thought about'.[189] The third position is a painful achievement, for it implies the acceptance of one's exclusion from something, though this something is the condition of the possibility of our existence (the creative couple) and of our capacity for reflection (not to be a partner in communication but to think of ourselves as partners in communication). This is what gives us the sense of a stable world and also the idea of another point of view as a creative space from which thoughts about relationships, as well as new ways of relating, can emerge. The baby wishes to control the mother and to believe theirs is the only possible relationship, to the detriment of all others. Therefore, the main Oedipal challenge to our narcissism and omnipotence is not just, as mentioned before,[190] the recognition of the father, the potent adult coming between baby and mother; the resolution of the Oedipus complex also involves the recognition of the parents as a *couple*, independent of the child. It is this challenge that can provide us with a capacity for thinking about ourselves and others in a way that allows difference and 'otherness' to exist.

The capacity for arguing and for thinking, so central to the Habermasian notion of discourse as emancipation, is seriously at risk if one does not recognize that which is not abstract thinking, but which makes thinking possible. In other words, the assumption of equality between subjects of discourse might work in the opposite direction to emancipation, in the sense that it might stop us from recognizing that thinking and discursive argumentation might be linked to an intersubjective world where ties of dependency and fragility are present from the start. The ideal of equality between partners in discourse might then work as a denial of our dependence, separateness and responsibility towards the vulnerability and fragility of others and ourselves.

Melanie Klein has been accused of overemphasizing aggression at the expense of other motives.[191] It is, however, important not to underestimate aggression and its disguises, especially when we are thinking of our mature capacities for recognizing the 'other' as equal and different in a process of argumentation and agreement. Indeed, we are all ready, to some extent, to own up to our envious or competitive attacks on our successful peers. In some ways, by these very attacks we strengthen the identification with our more successful colleagues at work or with our affluent neighbours. By recognizing our links of solidarity with these subjects, our fantasies of belonging to such an exclusive *coterie* are reinforced. It is not difficult here to imagine a dialogue or even an agreement between such subjects. It is when we think of the 'other' as unequal, as dependent, as fragile, and, more to the point, when we think of ourselves as dependent, fragile and *excluded*, that our more troubled conflicts and attacks come to the fore.

Psychoanalysis thinks about this situation in terms of the 'baby' and draws our attention to the fragile and dependent aspects in ourselves and how we have coped with those unbearable feelings. The bond that most clearly represents dependence as vulnerability and difference is the very primitive, absolute need of the baby for its mother. It is precisely this dimension of ourselves and others which is most frequently denied and which is, of course, most at risk in a generalization such as Habermas's on the equality of partners in communication. It is this dimension, that is, both the dependence and the love and gratitude associated with its recognition, that is addressed by Benhabib's idea of an ethics of care. It complements the aspiration for justice in terms of an *equality* among subjects with the need for a recognition of their *reciprocity*.[192] This is a recognition of the needs and the feelings that develop in the ongoing course of day-to-day relationships. These bonds also provoke, however, unbearable feelings of anger and rage. The baby cannot stand having to wait for the mother or depending on something that it does not control for its satisfaction. It will seek, from very early on, to attack the mother and deny her goodness. Let us therefore not romanticize this bond. As Alford points out, quoting Rivière, a contemporary colleague of Klein, the aggressive attack of the baby upon its mother is not 'a pretty picture':

> Loose motions, flatus and urine are all felt to be burning, corroding and poisonous agents. Not only the excretory, but all other physical functions are pressed into the service of the need for aggressive (sadistic) discharge and projection in fantasy. Limbs shall trample, kick and hit; lips, fingers and hands shall suck, twist, pinch; teeth shall bite, gnaw, mangle and cut; mouth shall devour, swallow and kill (annihilate); eyes kill by a look, pierce and penetrate.[193]

It is only by owning up to our own feelings of dependence, and to the hatred and love they provoke, that we can start to think in terms of an ethics of care, where we recognize that our bonds with others in the world involve not only rights amongst equals, but dependence amongst unequals. The recognition that autonomy is based upon solidarity is fundamental to an understanding of ethics. The idea of justice and a universalist moral and political theory has to account for something in ourselves and others that has not yet (and might never) achieve autonomy and responsibility. A dialogue with psychoanalysis, abandoned by Habermas, might enlarge a discourse ethics in order to encompass the 'other' as an other, that is, as an individuality which is different from our own, a creative couple that excludes me, a third position. Another possible dialogue that could also contribute to this broadening of the project of modernity would be a confrontation with Lyotard's postmodernist approach, which stresses the difference and the conflict. Following Levinas, Lyotard's approach to moral and political philosophy takes its impetus from the recognition of the 'other' as completely other than myself.

6

THE MOVE TO ETHICS: LYOTARD

Like Habermas, Lyotard's move to language is a move that leads him straight into the ethical domain. Indeed, Lyotard's critique of the grand narrative of modernity centres on the silence and the violence it imposes on other stories. His move to language as a heterogeneous multiplicity of conflicting language games is guided by the idea of the '*différend*', that is, the recognition that there always exist differences in language games, and that every difference is incommensurable and therefore never fully expressed by another language game. There is no final language game, no metanarrative that sums up the truth. With his idea of the '*différend*', Lyotard seeks to do justice to what cannot be said, what is necessarily excluded, forgotten and repressed in the encounter of different phrases, language games or perspectives. For Lyotard, language is a dispute, but a dispute that can never and should never be settled, as such a 'settlement' would mean the imposition, through power and violence, of one view over the others. In order to do justice to the '*différend*', Lyotard refuses to create a metanarrative about the heterogeneity of language. He wants to look for ways of creating and recovering a space where we can think about what has been forgotten or what cannot be said when we say something.

The main problem about such a position is, as we said before, that truth is equated with the imposition of one perspective over others: truth as the power to assert. When truth becomes identified with violence, however, there is no space left for critique or for the idea of justice to the repressed, which, one way or the other, Lyotard wants to maintain. As A. Honneth has argued,[194] there is an implicit contradiction in such a move, as Lyotard, the postmodern critic of truth, is actually claiming that there is a truth that has been repressed and which therefore must be heard, in the name of justice. Although Lyotard would probably question such a formulation of his position, in so far as it flattens the playfulness, diversity and ambiguity of language he wants to retain, he could not question the proximity of his work to the ideals of truth and justice present in the project of the philosophers of modernity. Still, the paradox and contradiction which Honneth questions are, for Lyotard, probably welcomed and enjoyed with the laughter of the sophist. The conversations Lyotard had with Thébaud on judgement and justice came out in France under the title *Au Juste*. In French, this had the double meaning of 'more exactly' and 'addressed to the just'. This mixture of truth and justice is another example of the mischievous tricks favoured by Lyotard, the disciple of Hermes. The English translator, faced with such an impossible task, managed to keep the ideas of the just and justice as linked to play and language games (*Just Gaming*). This is Lyotard's spirit, more so because the book is not 'just' a game, it is a reflection on justice which, at the same time, opens up new meanings with laughter. The laughter should not divert us, however, from realizing that the interest of an author such as Lyotard is that he is, maybe unwillingly and maybe even unwittingly (though he wishes precisely to allow for what is unintended and unknown), very close to the project of emancipation of the modernity tradition that he so criticizes.

Indeed, as we argued before,[195] Lyotard's critique of modernity, like that of Habermas, exposes the dangers of a technological society that purports to assert the truth of technology and efficiency as the only possible one. In *The Postmodern Condition*, Lyotard showed how the success of this type of rationality implies the loss of other competences, other 'savoirs-faire' which are excluded and forgotten in the process of expansion of this truth of 'modernity'. As Lyotard likes to recall,[196] however, it is Kant, the champion of modernity, who first fully recognized the diversity of the realms of reason, and differentiated between theoretical, practical and aesthetical rationalities, a differentiation which is also the key to Habermas's critique of positivism, scientism and the expansion of instrumental rationality. In this sense, when Lyotard, the postmodern herald, announces that 'there is no reason, only reasons',[197] Habermas and Kant would agree. It is the unchallenged expansion of scientific rationality which lies at the core of the nightmare of modernity as an iron cage.

The stress on the differentiated faculties of reason or forms of life recovers the domain of justice and morality from the systemization and impoverishment of instrumental rationality. The recognition of the different 'reasons' in language shows, for Lyotard, how justice does not follow a 'model', that is, how it does not derive from a representation worked out in theoretical discourse. Or, to use Lyotard's terms, the rules or the pragmatic regime of prescriptives do not follow from descriptions of what supposedly 'is'. There is a philosophical tradition, most clearly represented by Plato, which sought to define an idea of what justice is in order to bring society to conform to it.[198] Against it, Lyotard attempts to show that there are different phrases and linkages that are produced in different language games, and the mode of discourse of commands and prescriptions (the ethical domain) does not follow the propositional logic of theoretical discourse. The nightmare of modernity as an iron cage is that of instrumental rationality ruling alone and seeking to derive the rules of justice from scientific knowledge. Then the moral domain can be reduced to fit the rationality of the scientific and the technological, and, as Habermas frequently noted,[199] the logic of scientific and technological rationality views reality from the point of view of mastery and control.[200] This is a central and recurrent theme for Lyotard as well as for Habermas.

Indeed, from the beginning of his project, Habermas has sought to enlarge and strengthen the public space of discussion by stressing the interactive and communicative dimension of language as an alternative to instrumental rationality.[201] The move to language for Habermas was a continuation and development of this project. His *Theory of Communicative Action* takes the Kantian differentiation between various domains of rationality and shows how this differentiation does not happen in one's own mind, so to speak, or, in other words, how it is not the achievement of an isolated subject, but an on-going process of communication between partners in discourse. Isolated subjects for Habermas are not the starting-point of reflection, nor do they provide the grounds or the justification for discourse; rather, as linguistic subjects, they reveal the fundamental intersubjectivity of validity claims raised in discourse and show how the redemption of these claims can only be achieved by participants in it.

Lyotard produces a similar critique of the monological subject. For Lyotard, the story of modernity is a narrative centred on the subject of enunciation, proceeding through time as on an avenue of progress: accumulating knowledge and moving forward towards autonomy and self-determination. Lyotard seeks to challenge these principles of autonomy and self-determination as they are too enmeshed with an ideal of freedom based on an isolated subjectivity, the typical narrative of Western culture. He argues, in *Just Gaming* and in *The Postmodern Condition*, that a narrative has at least three poles or three pragmatic positions: the pole of the sender, that is, of the narrator; the pole of the addressee(s); and, finally, that of the world, which is the reference of the narrative.[202] In order to underline this point, Lyotard recalls the stories of the Cashinahua Indians in Peru and Brazil, as told by André Marcel d'Ans in his *Dits des Vrais Hommes*.[203] The Cashinahua narratives make us look at the other possible pragmatic positions, as in these tales, repeated time and again, the teller is not the author. Indeed, his only qualification for telling the story is that he has been its addressee before.[204] At the end, the teller tells us his or her name, but the Cashinahua proper name is also a way of localizing the teller in a network of kinship relations so that, in telling his or her name, the teller does not claim authorship but 'designates himself as someone who has been narrated by the social body, in a narrative that includes proper names and in which he has a place of his own. Among the stories he tells, there is also this story.'[205] There is no author of the narrative here, though this is not a denial of the variety of individual story-tellers. Indeed, some are more sought-after than others for their specific storytelling gifts. But the teller has no claims of autonomy regarding his tale. In fact, the emphasis is on the addressee and on the narrative which *includes* the teller in its tale. The idea of the subject and, more specifically, of the autonomy of a subject towards the story, is completely alien to a narrative which privileges tradition and the social body.

By tradition, Lyotard does not mean the uncritical conservation of the given; rather, it is a recognition of the time beating as the story goes on. The Western idea of progress of knowledge as the accumulation of contents, through conservation or critique, has no place here. The contents of the story, as well as the tellers and addressees, change and are forgotten. What is not forgotten is time itself, which is what the Western narrative, with its insistence on the narrators and on the 'progress' of knowledge forgets. The same beating of time can be seen in the case of 'popular' childish narratives, for instance nursery rhymes. As Lyotard says, '... nothing gets accumulated, that is, the narratives must be repeated all the time because they get forgotten all the time. But what does not get forgotten is the temporal beat that does not stop sending the narratives to oblivion.'[206]

There is, once again, a strange similarity between Lyotard's three pragmatic positions: the sender, the addressee(s) and the reference of the narrative and Habermas's three worlds opened up by communication. For Habermas as well, the subject of discourse is constituted within the three linguistic worlds created and made possible by the intersubjectivity of language: the external world of objects referred to by language, where a validity claim to truth is raised; the internal world of the individual subjects, where a validity claim to truthfulness is raised; and the social world of rules and norms for action, where a validity claim to justice is raised. All these worlds are linguistic, that is, intersubjective worlds, even the most 'private' of them, the internal world of one's own feelings and emotions. They have, as Lyotard points out, different rules, but for Habermas, they also point to the possibility of critique, in so far as participants in discourse, in raising different validity claims, agree to provide reasons for these claims, though, of course, these reasons can only be argued for in language. Still, for Habermas – and this is where the two authors part – the possibility of critique of, say, the ideal of autonomy as self-sufficiency, is opened up precisely by the recognition of the inevitable intersubjectivity of morality, and moreover, by the intersubjective, linguistic character of its possible justification. It is in language and through language that we can name the injustice promoted by the privileging of a narrative centred on a subject, and therefore we can recognize that autonomy is never self-sufficiency and isolation, as it necessarily involves solidarity between linguistic partners.[207]

This is where the difference of style and tactics between the two authors creates a real difference. We mentioned right at the beginning of this chapter how Honneth criticized Lyotard for using a notion of justice which he at the same time derided. It is not enough to use the sophist's stratagem and refuse to be cornered into just one possible use of language, for example, *either* rhetorical and ironical *or* theoretical and non-contradictory. The choice of a 'negative' type of critique, that is, of a type of writing that wishes to show the injustice done whilst at the same time refusing to develop a theory of justice, uses a constraining and extremely narrow definition of what theories and language can be. Lyotard does not wish to limit himself to this rhetorical, 'sceptical' corner.[208] On the other hand, because he identifies theories with domination, he is too prone to err on the side that he so criticizes, that is, he makes the mistake of generalizing what theories are and, in so doing, leaves no space for the recognition of the critical ('positive') capacities displayed in language through the interaction of participants or subjects (and objects) of discourse.

This is quite clear in Lyotard's critique of the autonomous reflective subject (the *cogito*), an idea which has shaped the Western tradition's ideals of freedom and justice. The resort to the Cashinahua narrative reminds us of the other possible positions in language and how obliged we are to the others in a narrative. This obligation becomes even clearer in Lyotard's use of the Jewish tradition, to which we shall come back later. The Cashinahua device illuminates the intersubjective dimension that must be there in order for us to be able to think at all, including the fiction of the author as the autonomous hero of Western narratives. This revelation, however, does not announce the death of the subject. Otherwise the death of 'Man', the subject of the Western narrative,[209] becomes the impossibility, from now onwards, of adopting the pragmatic position of the narrator. And this is Lyotard's weakness. There is, in Lyotard, a slide from the attack on the (isolated, autonomous) subject as the origin or the foundation of meaning to an attack on the very idea of a subject as a participant in communication. The same slide occurs from his questioning of truth understood as an unwarranted generalization of the truth of the scientific model, grounded once again in the fiction of an isolated subjectivity, to a questioning of truth, or 'modernity' in general. This makes it much more difficult to speak of the truth of a particular narrative (or phrase or sentence) or to use the notion of a subject, undoubtedly constituted in and through language, and therefore capable of contributing to a discourse on justice and truth.

Because Lyotard relinquishes these weapons, namely the recognition of the relevance of individual subjects reaching intersubjectively for the ideals of truth and justice, he remains close to his earlier mistake of an economy of desire. Even though he no longer resorts to an economy or energetic of libido or desire, the danger is there, in so far as language, especially in *The Differend*, can be seen as sentences or phrases without a sender, which thus become a sort of reality in segments: 'pieces' of reality. Even the sub-title of *The Differend* – 'Phrases in Dispute' – contributes to this, as it is much more reminiscent of the old logical positivist atoms of linguistic analyses than the Wittgensteinian theme of 'language games', which evokes the context, circumstances and participants involved in language. The detours and contortions Lyotard is then forced to go through in order to escape the dangers of becoming the 'author' of his own discourse,[210] are exemplary of the arbitrary limits he imposes on himself. Although 'Man' may be dead, I and you, in the here and now, are concrete individuals who should not and, indeed, cannot be ignored.

But if Lyotard is limited in his discourse by his refusal to develop the possibilities of critique opened up by the idea of communication between linguistic subjects – a communication and an understanding that take place in spite of irreconcilable differences – he is able to show some of the dangers contained in a position such as that of Habermas, which privileges the critical capacities displayed in language by a communication seeking to further understanding. The Habermasian ideal – though a counterfactual one – of a communication between equal and symmetrical partners in discourse seeking to justify, through reasons, the claims raised in language to truth, justice and freedom, without resort to force, is, for Lyotard, naïve. Indeed, for Lyotard, the ideals of symmetry, equality and transparency implicit in such a discourse constitute, in fact, a violence to the fundamental difference of the other participants in communication, even if we agree that the other is, like me, within language. In fact, Lyotard would go as far as Freud and claim that this 'otherness' is also within ourselves. Therefore the ideals – even counterfactual ones – of transparency, symmetry and equality are, for Lyotard, remnants of the philosophy of the subject. This might reveal Habermas's failure to move effectively away from the universalized 'I' of Kantian morality (the Categorical Imperative deriving from an 'I' that imagines itself in every other subject) to the intersubjectivity aimed at by his Discourse Ethics. An 'I' that absorbs the 'other' into itself, as if the other person were identical to the self, and as if this absorption were a form of justice, is really, by denying the 'otherness' of the other person, just affirming its own intrinsic superiority and exclusive right to being.

Lyotard uses the thought of the French Jewish philosopher Levinas with the purpose of highlighting this 'otherness' in other persons and also of showing how we relate to what he now calls this 'inhuman' dimension in ourselves.[211] Used at first as a way of showing the limitations of the narratives of the West, centred on the subject of discourse, the appeal to Levinas became more and more a way of showing that once we abandon the privileging of the subject of a narrative, we realize that a subject is always in relation to another person who remains other than ourselves. Such a realization is a recognition of the limitations of our philosophical tradition, centred on knowledge, which eventually transforms the other person into an object.

Levinas, whose philosophical work was formed by phenomenology, endorsed Heidegger's critique of Husserl in terms of the latter's reduction of our being-in-the-world to a relationship of knowledge. With Husserl, phenomenology became a methodology designed to achieve greater knowledge, rather than a disclosure of the ways meaning emerges in our consciousness of the world. In fact, Levinas' emphasis on Husserl's understanding of the intentionality of consciousness as something gesturing or reaching out to something other than itself, underlines how phenomenology can reveal that there is something *other* than consciousness, something that goes beyond synthesis and knowledge. This 'beyond', however, is not a world awaiting presentation and representation, but a recognition of an 'otherness' that escapes a reduction to knowledge. Husserl's phenomenology became an egology which reduced the very important insight into the 'lived body'(*Leib*) of consciousness, that is, the recognition of the various ways of pertaining and relating perceptually to the world, merely to the visual dimension, to a look and to an I(eye) that wishes to know. Heidegger argued that Husserl's phenomenological epistemology followed the Western tradition of a 'metaphysics of presence', that is, the Platonic project which equated truth with an intelligibility of presence. Such an equation, however, dismisses the temporal differentiation of the terms of the relationship of knowledge (subject and object) and assumes that an object can be effectively represented (and, as Heidegger has shown in his critique of technology, represented means mastered) in the here and now of atemporal presence.

Levinas goes even further than the hermeneutic critique. He tries to go behind Heidegger and the Greek tradition that inspired him by showing how Heidegger himself is still too enmeshed in the philosophy of presence by thinking of Being as a coming-into-presence (*Anwesen*).[212] In order to escape this intelligibility of presence, which he realizes is inevitable, in so far as language, and more specifi-cally, philosophical language is marked by the Hellenic tradition, Levinas draws on the Hebraic biblical tradition which, by speaking of God and His alterity, privi-leges the ethical dimension of our relationship to the 'other', and discloses the themes of concern and responsibility for this alterity. Such a relationship cannot be reduced to a relationship of knowledge, nor can we assume a fundamental equality of being between the participants: God and I. This is not, as is clear in Levinas' cri-tique of Buber, a plea for a treatment of the 'other' as 'a person', a 'Thou' as opposed to an 'It', an object.[213] The ethical recognition of the 'otherness' of the 'other' goes further in the sense that it seeks to recover a way of relating to the 'other' as an other forever beyond me, though this type of relationship has been almost buried and forgotten under the impact of knowledge and transparency. This is also a refusal to reduce time to a mere temporal flow, a recognition that the diachrony of time cannot be 'synthesized in the representation of qualitative con-tents bound to time'.[214] We think of time as atoms of presence to our consciousness, but Levinas stresses the irreducible infinity of time which can never be totalized and contained into a past, a present and a future.[215]

The fundamental point to our discussion is precisely this unequivocal refusal of a reduction of the 'other' to the same, a refusal that stresses the 'otherness' of the 'other' and the impossibility of reducing the infinity of time to a flow of temporal units. As Levinas says in a passage that might have been written as a critique of Habermas (though it was not), we can turn to language in order to show that the relationship between participants goes beyond a represented content that remains identical with itself. But philosophical language, so imbued with rationalism and knowledge, 'interprets this otherness as the mutual discovery of interlocutors within the *Same* ...'. And then, 'The questions and answers which make up an "exchange of ideas" could just as well be held within a *single* consciousness.'[216] Against this ideal of symmetry, Levinas proposes to think of the relationship with the 'other' as a 'vertical' face-to-face, a way of drawing our attention to what is forced upon us, namely the recognition of the 'other' as other than ourselves.

This face-to-face relationship is not merely the call for information about the 'other', as the rationalist's emphasis on comprehension and knowledge would have it. It also calls our attention to a proximity that exists before representation, before knowledge. In fact, a face refuses to be reduced to an eye, that is, it refuses to be made solely into a subject or an object of a relationship of knowledge. According to Levinas, it provokes a dual response: a temptation to kill this 'other' who imposes himself upon me, and a summons not to kill ('Thou shall not kill'), which marks the entrance to an ethical relationship of proximity to the 'other', the 'human fraternity'.[217] It is impossible here not to think of Melanie Klein's dual response to the mother as the wish to devour and the gratitude that comes with the recognition of the 'other'. She also shows how this face-to-face is the most basic human response, one that does not wait for the more mature resolution of the Oedipus complex, as it happens from the very start of life.

The rage and the outrage felt at the thought that an 'other' person is necessary for our physical and emotional survival, creates, as we mentioned, a murderous attack on the object and a desire to deny this object. Unless we recognize, however, in the adult, male, autonomous subject the vulnerable and clumsy baby who cannot exist without the (m)'other', we cannot give due weight to the feelings of love (as well as hatred) created by this relationship which will shape and colour our 'mature' relations with the world (as, for instance, in Hobbes' fantasy of mushrooms springing from the earth and in Habermas's ideal of justice as a discourse between equal partners). The capacity for dealing with the ambivalence towards the other is a measure of our capacity for recognizing our belonging to what Levinas calls, rather unfortunately, a 'fraternity',[218] but also, more felicitously, an ethical community.

Given the difficulty, or resistance, as Freud calls it, to accept the bonds of dependency on an 'other' who cannot be reduced to oneself, it is important to try to understand what particular response this recognition imposes upon us. A. J. Vetlesen[219] has opposed Levinas' understanding of the 'other' to Sartre's, an opposition that, on Sartre's side, vividly illustrates the *hatred* these feelings evoke, and to what extent even a thinker as fully committed as Sartre to the idea of freedom and authenticity as that which makes us human, can go in order to reject this dependence.

Sartre's literary and philosophical works have made famous the view that 'Hell is the others': the others constitute a threat and a limit to my personal freedom. Indeed, for Sartre, the experience of the 'other' fills me with shame as I have to conceive a vision of myself in terms of the way in which another sees me. The 'other' does a violence to me in exposing the limits of my knowledge and my control. In other words, the 'other' forces me to accept that I am not the only master, that I am not, as psychoanalysis would put it, omnipotent in my narcissism. I must accept that there is an unknown, something that escapes me; this is made clear by the presence of another person who has a knowledge of myself which forever escapes my control.

To be fair, for Sartre, the 'other' is also a promise of freedom, as only the other person, as a free consciousness, can give me the recognition that I seek but which I never find. The painful recognition of the necessity of the 'other' has found in Sartre the traditional solution of modern philosophy. Because the 'other' constitutes a threat to and a confinement of my personal freedom, I need to transform this 'otherness' into the same. The 'other' – who forces me to stare into the unknown as my limit – is, then, an 'other' *just like me*, someone who also resents my imposing on him an 'outside', that is, a recognition that there is a knowledge of himself that he does not possess. Thus, I also set a limit to *his* freedom and he resents me just as I resent him. The idea that there is an 'other' who is not like myself is lost, as the encounter of subjects becomes the fight for power over knowledge. Sartre is closer to Husserl's egology than to Heideggerian hermeneutics. In his quest to go back to the real encounter between concrete individuals which, he felt, Heidegger's ontology did not meet, Sartre went back to the Cartesian *cogito*, though this *cogito* now, of necessity, reveals the existence of the 'other'. But the 'other' is not truly 'other';

rather, another subject just like myself. He does reveal the limits of my conscious-ness,[220] but these limits are 'similar' to mine, irrespective of the claim that they are unknown. Freedom, then, is the freedom of the isolated subject, and the recogni-tion of my dependence on the m(other) or on the 'fraternity' of human beings can only fill me with shame (at the loss of my omnipotent self-image) or with hatred for this 'other'.

Levinas, however, is able to point in another direction, by stressing that the obli-gation towards the 'other' comes *before* freedom. He does not start from the *cogito*, be it the simple Cartesian one, or the more complex, politically responsible, tormented and anxious Sartrean one. We start from a relationship to the 'other' that can never be reduced to the knowledge or mastery I can gain over this 'other'. For Sartre, the 'original fall' is the necessity of my recognition of the 'other' as a limit to my freedom. Freud famously commented on the three blows to our narcissism delivered first by Copernicus, then by Darwin and finally by psychoanalysis. The facts that the Earth is not the centre of the universe, that man is not different from other animals and that the ego is not the master in his own house are indeed terrible blows. But narcissism can try to reappropriate to itself the idea of the unconscious by making it into an extension of the solitary consciousness, an idea very distant from Freud's. The stress of Melanie Klein on object-relations shows how narcis-sism seeks to avoid the recognition of the 'other', and how this denial is mostly unconscious.

This is the real meaning of Freud's theory, not some idealization of the uncon-scious as that which is non-rational, and therefore not incorporated by the human-ist tradition. The unconscious aggression and destruction of our links with and separateness from the 'other' is what we do not want to see under the idealization of the libidinal impulses. In Sartrean terms, the 'other' is the limit to my 'free-dom', but in Freudian and Kleinian terminology, the 'other' is the limit to my nar-cissism. The recognition of the 'other', especially as a couple that excludes me, enrages me but it also creates the possibility of 'another way of looking at things', a reflection on myself and my relationships from another position: what Britton called the 'third position'.[221] It creates a space where imagination and creativity (the unknown which surpasses me) are recognized, and the dyad subject–object placed within a wider context.

For Levinas, there is no initial fall but there is an original call. This is the 'Thou shall not kill' of biblical tradition which reveals the care and concern we must show for the 'other' as an 'other' who refuses to be the same and whom we have a responsibility to look after as an 'other'. Indeed, Levinas is fond of quoting Alyosha Karamazov: 'We are all responsible for everyone else – but I am more responsible than all the others'.[222] The original sin, for Levinas – as for Klein – is the denial of the fundamental indebtedness and obligation to the 'other'.

It is important to stress that, for psychoanalysis, narcissism is the real evil genius. It can distort our view of knowledge, even of psychoanalytically-inspired knowledge. The recognition that the ego is not master in its house does not deny the powers of reason, but it changes our understanding of what reason and knowledge can aspire to be. The resolution of the Oedipus complex should be the beginning of a less omnipotent view of the world, a recognition of the 'others' as brothers. The death of the father should be a metaphor for the end of our infantile omnipotent wishes to have it all. The problem is how this pact between these brothers can easily become the pact between the exclusive members of a certain group, thus creating the monstrous illusion of becoming the ideal father in the guise of a diverse community. The brothers here are busily working within the confines of the paranoid-schizoid position, excluding what is not the same – the sisters and the mother to start with – and also those who threaten their self-idealization by possessing something they want and do not have. Once again, it is important to remember that these mechanisms are not a male prerogative, as feminists can build such an enclave with the same enthusiasm. The feminine world is not exempt from aggression, destruction and envy, and women have the same capacity as men for denying their envious attacks. That is why the added layer of meaning to the early Oedipus complex of Kleinian theory is so illuminating. It shows how the 'other' that lies outside the exclusive 'relationship-à-deux' is a couple, that is, a creative union which I am not. I can introject this object as a child introjects the model of the father or the mother as that which it wishes to be. But the introjection of the fertile couple is the recognition that thinking and creativity involve the 'other', the respect and care for the intersubjective world.

It is in this light that the critique of Habermas by Lyotard is so important. It is a reminder of the dangers of the ideals of equality and symmetry as an illusion of the same. The ideas of infinity and of the 'other', clearly borrowed from Levinas, are very helpful. In Lyotard's terms, they are the 'inhuman' (again the laughter of the sophist), that is, they are that which escapes identification with the same, though more often than not, the same is appealingly depicted as that which makes us all human. Lyotard would say that what makes us human is the inhuman in us, that is, that which resists all our attempts to reduce 'otherness' to the same.

If Lyotard were saying that there is no way we can approach this unknowable, as it is definitely 'other' and forever unknowable, then he would indeed be parting from the project of modernity. But this is no longer what Lyotard is saying. He distinguishes between two types of the inhuman: the inhuman as the dehumanization that the system of instrumental rationality achieves, by promoting a type of knowledge that reduces everything to information, and the inhuman as that which escapes the system, as an 'otherness' that refuses to become the same.[223] The example of the inhuman that Lyotard chooses is, interestingly enough, the 'nature' present in the helpless child before the achievement of maturity through culture and education:

> Shorn of speech, incapable of standing upright, hesitating over the objects of its interest, not able to calculate its advantages, not sensitive to common reason, the child is eminently the human because its distress heralds and promises things possible. Its initial delay in humanity, which makes it the hostage of the adult community, is also what manifests to this

community the lack of humanity it is suffering from, and which calls on it
to become more human.' (Lyotard, 1991, p.4).

It is to this childhood, still present in all of us adults, though for the most part forgotten or tamed, that Lyotard draws our attention, as a way of resisting the overpowering forces of the other type of the inhuman, which dehumanizes us. This is
the task of justice for Lyotard: to bear witness, to remember and to create spaces
through art and writing for this indeterminate, this 'other', this unconscious primitive nature, epitomized by the helpless baby. The achievement of reason even as
differentiated forms of rationality – theoretical, moral-practical and aesthetic – can
only be realized when consciousness, knowledge and will do not erase and eradicate the traces of this inhuman. A moral reason must show its indebtedness and its
obligation to that which it is not, but which makes its achievement as moral reason
possible. This is not a mystical idealization of the inhuman as the unknowable, but
a reminder that any type of knowledge which does not allow for this 'otherness',
does, in effect, attack it and therefore transforms itself into a type of knowledge
that does not really know.

Interestingly enough, in the papers collected in *The Inhuman*, Lyotard uses the
Freudian idea of 'working-through' as an alternative to a type of knowledge that
seeks to master the object. As we mentioned in the first chapter, the idea of working-through was so novel that Strachey, the English translator, found himself
struggling with his choice of words. The idea of becoming 'conversant with what
is unknown' is so distant from the traditional ideal of knowledge as mastery of the
object represented, that Strachey translated 'unknown' by 'what (the patient) has
now become acquainted with'.[224] Lyotard uses this idea of working through as a
way of showing how a different type of knowledge is possible, a knowledge which
is not separate from suffering or feeling, a knowledge that indeed bears the marks
of pain and pleasure.

For Klein, Bion and the contemporary Kleinians, thinking cannot be dissociated
from our very concrete emotional experiences of the world. It is a capacity for
making links which can be traced back to the very early, pre-verbal, 'non-
reasonable' experiences with the mother as a vulnerable baby. Thought does not
come 'after', as a mature achievement of reason. Thought and reason bear also the
unthought and the unreasonable, and it is only by becoming 'conversant' with the
pain and suffering as well as with the love and pleasure that we experience with the
'other' that we can pay tribute to our mature rational capacities as a human. This is
not a solitary but an intersubjective achievement.

This is the fundamental contribution Lyotard and psychoanalysis can provide to
Habermas's project of modernity. The challenge is how to contribute to the project
of modernity conceived as a theory of justice which is not instrumental. The idea of
an ethical reason which relies solely on reasons rather than on force is, undoubtedly, that which can defend and safeguard the heterogeneity of our multi-cultural
societies. This project, however, which is indeed the project of the Enlightenment,
can only proceed when, as Lyotard ironically puts it, it 'advances backwards'

(1991, p.3) in the direction of the 'other' and of the unknown. The danger is a tendency for the system to overcome a knowledge of the indeterminate, the unconscious, the childish and the vulnerable and to transform it into the already known, into the same, the calculable and the instrumental. On the other hand, it is also important to maintain, against the tendency of postmodernity, to define all knowledge as a form of domination, that it is possible and indeed vital to recognize our indebtedness to the 'other' and our insertion in the intersubjective world. And, as Habermas has so rightly shown, the capacity, displayed in language, for understanding and recognition of the 'other' as a partner in discourse, indeed provides grounds for hope for our capacity for maintaining dialogue and further understanding. But without an understanding of what in us and in language seeks to flatten and destroy this capacity, either by force *or* by the kind of 'reasonable' reflection that transforms the 'other' into the same, we cannot hope to achieve true understanding.

This is not a matter of creating two different types of thinking: an ethics of justice, where the principle of equality would be upheld, and an ethics of care, where the empathy and capacity for imagining, understanding and looking after what is unknown, unformulated or fragile, would be provided. The challenge that both psychoanalysis and modernity pose is how to rethink the principle of universalization, so fundamental to the Discourse Ethics of Habermas, as a principle that must include the vulnerable, the unthought and the unknown. The idea that partners in communication ideally provide arguments where the better reasons prevail, concentrates on our mature capacities for arguing. These capacities, however, as has been said against Piaget's developmental stages,[225] are particularly developed in our scientific and technological cultures, and this fact should alert us to the dangers of misusing these capacities to forget what is not so easily articulated or verbalized. Without this understanding, we are in danger of forgetting the 'other', who might be the most affected by our actions. The Habermasian assumption, even as a counterfactual one, of a discourse among equal partners forgets that we are and must also be responsible for those who are not present, cannot be made present as they are not yet born, or are unable to speak, unequal or unknown. This does not mean a refusal of the ideal of justice, but a recognition, *à la* Freud, that the death of omnipotence does not kill knowledge, only the omnipotent ideal of knowledge as absolute.

Psychoanalysis, and most particularly the Kleinian emphasis on the destructive and envious aspects of our psychological make-up, can help us understand how underneath an ideal of justice an injustice is being done: how the brothers of *Totem and Taboo* can indeed still be under the spell of the omnipotent father, now introjected as 'we', the real brothers or the chosen people. Then the 'other' is the threat, and I have to build up my defences against this unbearable difference, the savage outside. Levinas' political view that it is Israel's duty to recognize the Palestinians is an example that should help us see how a politics of justice, based on our obligation to and respect for the 'other' could proceed. But the mystery of the

98

'other' as also that which we wish to kill is important to bear in mind if we want to understand our wish not to know and to destroy knowledge and humanity.

Indeed, without it, we are in danger of idealizing and romanticizing the 'other' as more real than anything else. In this romantic vein, madness becomes the truth and the baby becomes solely an expression of love, with the mother–baby couple as the symbol of happiness and plenitude. This is a complete denial of the destruction, similar to the manic reparation which is characteristic of the paranoid position. The baby is not only vulnerability, as any mother knows. The despair and the rage experienced by all mothers are evidence enough of the power and the difficulties of a relationship that involves not just love and gratitude, but rage and destruction as well. What is very difficult for the baby (and for the adult) to accept is that there is another, more 'real' (or fertile) couple, that there is a world outside ourselves which we wish to destroy. The acknowledgement of this exclusion and the feelings it provokes are what mark our entrance into the world of others, where creative thought and reflection become possible. Kleinian psychoanalysis emphasizes both: the envious and destructive impulses, as well as our capacity for repairing and restoring the love and affection. This capacity becomes *caritas,* real concern for the 'other', only when it recognizes the damage done. This approach provides us with an understanding of how this 'otherness' can work against our more conscious wishes for respect, justice and knowledge, and how there is not a clear split between the good and the bad, as there is in the traditional version that sees the 'other' as 'the bad' and in the romantic version that sees the 'other' as 'the good'. The recognition of the power and pervasiveness of this destructiveness enables us to see how difficult it is to maintain a proximity to what we do not know, but with which we must familiarize ourselves. It is this challenge, which we faced before as babies, and which we must face again forever, which makes thinking possible. On this 'inhuman' – to paraphrase both Habermas and Lyotard – rests the humanity of our human relationships.[226]

NOTES

1   The lectures given by Foucault at PUC/RJ under the title 'Truth and Juridical Forms' were recorded and the translated typescript was published internally by Cadernos da PUC (Foucault, 1974).
2   For an illuminating discussion of the scientificity of psychoanalysis, see M. Rustin (1991).
3   *The Assault on Truth* (1985) is the best example. There have been others, more or less scholarly documented. A recent example starts from the proliferation of cases of adults who, through a specific form of therapy which is neither Freudian nor psychodynamic in its orientation, recover a questionable memory of their abuse as children. Newspapers have then tried to make a case against all forms of therapy, especially those which claim (as psychoanalysis does) that early experiences in childhood are fundamental for adult capacities.
4   R. Bernstein made these terms popular in his book *Beyond Objectivism and Relativism*.
5   Lyotard (1986), pp.91-2, my italics. The theme and the argument are not new. To name but the most famous, Adorno and Horkheimer (1979) had waged a war on reason along the same lines.
6   Adorno, the author with Horkheimer of *The Dialectic of the Enlightenment* was a formidable critic of reason. Marcuse, also part of the Frankfurt School, was the author of *Reason and Revolution* and the mentor of the 1960s revolution in the United States.
7   Weber (1978), p.141.
8   Habermas first used the *querelle* to this purpose in his acceptance of the Adorno Prize in 1980 (translated as 'Modernity versus Postmodernity' in *New German Critique, 22* (1981).
9   Baudelaire (1964): 'By modernity I mean the ephemeral, the fugitive, the contingent, the half of art whose other half is the eternal and the immutable.'
10   In the 1960s, in Marxist circles, it seemed crucial to define these 'objective relations', as this definition helped to clarify the level of autonomy (if any) of the world of ideas *vis-à-vis* the economic world. In order to soften the impact of the more economic works of Marx (*Capital*, 1867, 1885, 1894), the reading of the younger, more 'philosophically' minded Marx (*Economic and Philosophical Manuscripts*, 1844) was recommended.
11   'But as absolute knowledge, reason assumes a form so overwhelming that it not only solves the initial problem of a self-reassurance of modernity, but solves it *too well*. The question about the genuine self-understanding of modernity gets lost in reason's ironic laughter. For reason has now taken over the place of fate and knows that every event of essential signification has *already* been decided.' (Habermas, 1987b, p.42.)
12   'Just as the transitory, momentary and contingent can only be half of art that requires of its other half the constant, timeless and universal, so also the historical consciousness of *modernité* presupposes the eternal as its antithesis ... timeless beauty is nothing other than the idea of beauty in the status of past experience, an idea created by human beings themselves and continually abandoned.' H.R. Jauss, 'Literarische Tradition und gegenwärtiges Bewusstein der Modernität' in Jauss (1970), quoted by Frisby (1985), p.16.
13   See Bernstein (1983).

14   Lyotard's argument, clearly reminiscent of the Frankfurt School tradition, shows that reason, when transformed into efficiency, does not allow the question of the meaning of the extermination.

15   In 'A Review of Gadamer's *Truth and Method* ' in Dallmayr and McCarthy (1977), Habermas says: 'Language is *also* a medium of domination and social force. It serves to legitimize relations of organized power. In so far as the legitimations do not articulate the power relations whose institutionalization they make possible, in so far as these relations merely manifest themselves in the legitimations, language is also ideological'. The idea of a distorted use of communication implies an ideal of a non-distorted use which Habermas will later call the 'ideal speech situation'. In order to avoid the inevitable criticism of idealism, Habermas claimed that such an ideal is implicit in every actual use of speech by the very fact that we speak and expect people to speak truthfully, legitimately and truefully as a basis for possible understanding. This is, however, a counterfactual claim, and Habermas even calls it an 'illusion', in order to underline that the truth, legitimacy and veracity of the actual statements are not at stake here. What is crucial is the necessary assumption that we expect others and ourselves to be speaking truthfully, legitimately and truefully as a basis for understanding and even as a basis for lies and deceits (Habermas 1977, and see below, Chapter 2, which discusses Habermas's linguistic turn).

16   'The propositionally contentless speech about Being has, nevertheless, the illocutionary sense of demanding resignation to fate. Its practical-political side consists in the perlocutionary effect of a diffuse readiness to obey in relation to an auratic but indeterminate authority.' (Habermas 1987b, p.140).

17   Derrida (1986). See also Habermas's critique of Derrida (Habermas 1987b).

18   See for instance P. Mendelson (1979) and P. Ricoeur (1973).

19   Gadamer (1981, 1987).

20   Lyotard explicitly refers, on these issues, to Merleau-Ponty's *Humanisme et Terreur* and *La Phénoménologie de la Perception*. I asked Lyotard once whom he regarded as a major influence on his work. Th first name mentioned was Merleau-Ponty's.

21   Lyotard (1986).

22   Some of this work has been reprinted in Lyotard (1993).

23   Lyotard (1974, 1983). Wellmer (1981) comments on this return to positivism: 'This bizarre postmodernist conception ... betokens both a regression to Adorno and Nietzsche and in the same breath a sidestep from Adorno to Positivism. For in substituting the will ("in the sense of wanting what is possible") for an "attitude which is regulated by the edifice and artificiality of representation" and with the dissolution of semiotics into "energetics", Lyotard's postmodernism becomes indistinguishable from behaviourism'. (p.40).

24   See Laplanche and Pontalis (1980). This is also a fundamental tenet of object-relations and particularly Kleinian psychoanalytical theory (Isaacs, 1989). We shall return to this discussion in Chapter 4.

25   The idea of a science that would combine causal explanation with meaningful understanding goes back to Max Weber and his idea of 'explanatory understanding', that is, his wish for a scientific point of view that would still understand the social world of values. Habermas's point is reminiscent of this tradition, but it places a stronger emphasis on language and interpretation. Ricoeur (1973), in his comparison between Gadamer and Habermas, speaks of a 'depth hermeneutics', a hermeneutic approach that seeks to go beyond the level of interpretation in order to understand and thereby transform the distortions of power.

26   This criticism is not restricted to Freudian-inspired literature. One of the most famous critics of Piaget was Vygotsky (1979), and Chomskyan psycholinguistics have also challenged Piagetians (Piatelli-Palmarini, 1979). For a brilliant review and discussion of the psychological and sociological problems of the work of Piaget, see Buck-Morss (1987). Her critique follows the Frankfurt School tradition.

27   'Open the supposed body and lay out all its surfaces: not only the skin with each of its folds, wrinkles. scars, with its great velvety spaces, attached to it the scalp and its mop of hair; the tender

pubic fur, the nipples, the nails, the transparent corns under the heel, the light fripperies, grated with lashes, with eyelids, but also open and pin down, reveal the great labia, the lesser labia with their blue mucous covered network, dilate the diaphragm of the anal sphincter, cut the black tunnel of the rectum and flatten it, then the colon, then the caecum, henceforth a ribbon with a tattered and shit-spattered surface, with your dressmaker's scissors opening the leg of an old trouser, go on, bring to the light of day the supposed interior of the small intestine, of the jejunum, of the ileum, of the duodenum, or maybe from the other end slit into the mouth at the corners, dig out the tongue at its deepest root and split it, pin out the wings of the bats of the palate and its damp basements, open the trachea and make it the skin of a hull under construction; armed with lancets and the finest pincers, take apart and set down the bundles and bodies of the encephalon; and then the entire circulatory system intact flat on a great mattress, and the lymphatic system, and disassemble and place end to end all the fine bony pieces of the wrist, of the ankle, with all the layers of nervous tissue that surround the aqueous humour and the cavernous body of the penis, extract the great muscles, the great dorsal networks, spread them out like smooth sleeping dolphins. Do the work that the sun does when you sun-bathe, the job that pot does.' (Lyotard, 1974), pp. 9–10.

28 See above and Habermas (1978).
29 See, in this context, the recent controversy in psychoanalytical circles on the meaning of a clinical fact (Tuckett, 1994). Striving for an integration of various, sometimes radically opposed theories, some psychoanalysts have claimed that taping and possibly even filming the session might help settle these disputes, as if these transcriptions could tell the ultimate meaning of the psychoanalytical interaction. The Kleinian group, given its particular emphasis on the conscious and unconscious communications that are taking place during a the session in the transference and countertransference, oppose this view. E. O'Shaughnessy, for instance, argued that psycho-analysis must recognize the intrinsic intersubjective exchange that takes place in the setting, an exchange that cannot be recorded by an objective lens, nor by a neutral observer (in Tuckett, 1994).
30 Habermas (1978), p.234, italics mine.
31 Freud, 'Remembering, Repeating and Working Through' (*SE XII*, p.155), my italics. See also note 1, same page. The correspondence of James Strachey with his wife Alix (Meisel and Kendrick, 1986) is extremely helpful to an understanding of the problems surrounding the translation of Freud's work. It shows how the first translators were struggling not just with the originality of Freud's ideas, but also with trying to make psychoanalytical ideas more 'acceptable' to English scientific and artistic circles, thus sometimes departing from the original text.
32 P. Heimann, originally a Kleinian and later a member of the Independent group, wrote the classic 'On Countertransference' in 1949–50 (Heimann, 1989).
33 Freud, 'Recommendations to Physicians Practising Analysis', *SE XII* and King (1989).
34 P. Grosskurth (1986).
35 See Laplanche and Pontalis (1980) and also Chapter 4.
36 J. Benjamin, (1994), p.231.
37 Lyotard (1988), p.xiii.
38 Lyotard (1986), p.66.
39 Ibid, p.66.
40 Habermas (1979), p.1, my italics.
41 The best examples would be the *Tractatus* itself or Russell's and Moore's analyses, as criticized in the *Philosophical Investigations*, pp.60, 63, 64.
42 Wittgenstein (1974), p.65.
43 Ibid. pp.66–70, 92, 97: 'We are under the illusion that what is peculiar, profound, essential, in our investigation resides in its trying to grasp the incomparable essence of language.'; p.124: '[Philosophy] cannot give [language] any foundation either.'
44 Habermas (1975, 1970b).
45 Chomsky (1970), p.3.

46 Habermas speaks of 'die generative Fähigkeit' in 'Sprachspiel ...' (1975).
47 Hymes (1970).
48 See, for instance, the radical criticism of the idea of a 'deeper essence of language developed by Baker and Hacker (1984), eminent Wittgenstein scholars who wrote a detailed analysis of the *Philosophical Investigations* (183a, 1983b).
49 Wittgenstein (1984), p.150.
50 Habermas (1975).
51 Habermas (1979, 1984, 1987a).
52 Wittgenstein (1974), p.241.
53 Habermas (1975).
54 Dallmayr (1972), McCarthy (1978).
55 Austin (1975).
56 Austin (1962).
57 Felman (1983), p. 63: 'How indeed, might one find the truth of that which, as such, deconstructs the criterion of truth itself? Austin's distinction ends up subverting itself.'
58 Habermas (1971). For the full quotation see n. 62 below.
59 Habermas (1973).
60 Habermas (1973), McCarthy (1978).
61 Havel (1985).
62 Habermas (1971), p.120: 'On this unavoidable fiction rests the humanity of intercourse among men who are still men, that is, men who have not become totally alien as subjects in their self-objectivations.' ('Auf dieser unvermeidlichen Fiktion beruht die Humanität des Umgangs unter Menschen, d. h. in ihren Selbstobjektivationen noch nicht sich als Subjekten vollig fremd geworden sind.').
63 Habermas (1979).
64 Searle (1972, 1979).
65 For a critique of Searle's principle, see Stampe (1975) and Steuerman (1985).
66 Thompson (1982).
67 For Freud, an instinct had an aim (its satisfaction), an object ('the thing in regard to which or through which the instinct is able to achieve its aim') and a source (the body: 'the somatic processes which occur in an organ or part of the body and whose stimulus is represented in mental life by an instinct') (Freud, 'Formulations on the Two Principles of Mental Functioning', *SE XII*, pp.122-3). By emphasizing the relation to the object of the instinct, Klein and the 'object-relations' theory moved away from the model of psychoanalysis as a natural science. See also below, Chapter 4.
68 Freud, op. cit.; Laplanche and Pontalis (1980); Ricoeur (1965, 1970).
69 Piontelli (1992).
70 Recent research in child development seems to support and confirm the psychoanalytical approach. See, for instance, Alvarez (1992), Stern (1985), and Trevarthen (1986).
71 Bion (1977), Winnicott (1976).
72 Bion, (1988), O'Shaughnessy (1988).
73 Alvarez (1992), Bion (1977, 1988), Rustin (1991).
74 Arendt (1984).
75 Lyotard (1988).
76 The present becomes an atom of time, separated and distinct from time itself: 'For a lifetime can be divided into innumerable parts that do not depend on each other in any way. The fact that I existed a short while ago does not imply that I must exist at present unless some other cause re-creates me, as it were, in the present moment or, in other words, conserves me.' (Descartes 1998), p.41; (1970), p. 297.
77 There is another twist to the tale: Lyotard (1988), p.8 recalls that in the version given by Aulus-Gellius, the dispute between Protagoras and Euathlus is held in front of a tribunal: 'It could be retranscribed as follows: Protagoras: "If you win (against me), you will have won; if you lose

(against me) even if you say you always lose (against others), then you will still have won. The judges are perplexed." But then Euathlus puts time on *his* side and says: "If I lose (against you), I will have lost; if I win (against you), even if I say I always lose, then I will still have lost".' Lyotard concludes: 'The judges decide to put off their pronouncement until later. The history of the world cannot pass a last judgement. It is made out of judged judgements.'

78 Freeman (1983). See also the film, *Margaret Mead and Samoa*, CINETEL Productions, Sydney. I am grateful to Adam Kuper for drawing this case to my attention, and for his wonderful paper, which I use in the above discussion.

79 Kuper (1989).

80 *Antilogic* was the probable title of one of Protagoras treatises. Plato refers to it in the *Theaetetus*.

81 Freud, 'The Unconscious' in *On Metapsychology*, Standard Edition, vol. *xiv*.

82 'When a primary process is allowed to take its course in connection with elements belonging to the system Pcs, it appears 'comic' and it excites laughter' (Freud, 'The Unconscious', *SE XIV*, p.186). We also know of Freud's particular interest in jokes and their relationship to the unconscious.

83 Lyotard, 'Answering the Question: What is Postmodernism?' in *The Postmodern Condition* (1986).

84 Lyotard (1986, 1986b).

85 Rorty's reading of Lyotard follows these lines (Rorty, 1985).

86 Freud, 'The Unconscious', *SE XIV*.

87 Particularly in *The Postmodern Condition*.

88 See n.77, above.

89 Once again Baudelaire's definition of *modernité* as the contingent and the eternal comes to mind (Baudelaire, 1984 and Chapter 1, above).

90 See, for instance, J. Cohen (1989), p.496: '... a life world which has, however imperfectly and partially, institutionalized universalistic principles to guarantee freedom and justice is, to be sure, ours, but this historically contingent fact does not render claims to democratic legitimacy particularistic. On the contrary, claims to democracy and rights which can be discursively redeemed reveal the particularistic and pernicious dimensions of those forms of life, existing within a modernized lifeworld that are incompatible with a political way of life guided by the principles of justice. Against the liberal claims to absolute neutrality, the neo-communitarian is quite correct – democratic and liberal institutions embody norms and principles that are often substantive and comprise a political way of life. But this is the *advantage* of an *incomplete* ethico-political concept of justice ...'

91 J. Steiner (1985). See also Britton *et al* (1989).

92 Habermas (1970a, 1978).

93 Habermas (1970a, 1978).

94 Kuhn (1970).

95 Wittgenstein (1974) pp.133, 144: 'I have changed his *way of looking at things*.' For a riveting discussion of philosophy as therapy, see Edwards (1982).

96 Freud, 'Remembering, Repeating and Working Through', *SE XII*, and also above, Chapter 1.

97 Habermas (1984, 1987a).

98 Lyotard, (1986), pp.19-23.

99 J.-L. Nancy, from a very different perspective to that of Habermas, also seems to agree that reason in its practical use, that is, in judging, displays its universal dimension. Every time I judge, he claims without fear of the paradox, it is the last judgement. In the practical instance of critical judgement, reason posits itself as unconditioned: it must interminably invent the indeterminable. 'Thus the idea is not an Idea of reason projected in the guise of a fictional *telos*, but the Idea is reason outside of itself, of determining rationality, and it dares to *judge*. Judgement is the risk of reason .... I don't judge here in order to verify subsequently the agreement of the course I chose with the facts of experience, but in judging I venture a "reason" (or unreason) which is judged by what it attempts or risks ... . I am judged by the world I attempt, which I am willing to risk and not

by the established world. It is my last judgement at every attempt.' ('Dies Irae' in Derrida *et al.* 1985).

100 Honneth (1995a, 1995b) makes this point.

101 Freud, *An Autobiographical Study, SE XX*; see also Ricoeur (1965), Rieff (1960).

102 Steuerman (1988), Meisel and Kendrick (1986).

103 Ricoeur (1965), p.82; (1970), p.72.

104 Freud, *The Unconscious, SE XIV*, p.175. Also Wollheim (1973) and Rieff (1960).

105 'Instinct' is the accepted English translation of two different German words, *Trieb* and *Instinkt*. *Trieb* denotes the pressure exerted (*treiben* means to push), irrespective of the aim of the object, whereas *Instinkt* suggests the behaviour common to all members of a certain species. Laplanche and Pontalis (1980) argued that the translation of instinct for both words blurs this important distinction. For Freud, *Trieb* (the French *pulsion*) does not have a stable object.

106 John Huston's film on Freud, *Freud, the Secret Passion*, is an example of this. Jean-Paul Sartre wrote the original script for the film, which was later revised and substantially transformed (see J.-P. Sartre, *The Freud Scenario*, 1985). Freud's own views on the meaning of the primal scene tend to confirm this view (see Ricoeur, 1970, p.161: '... the theme of the "primitive scene" that Freud will always try to connect with real memories, even after he has given up its first expression in the supposed scene of the child's seduction by the adult.').

107 The work of Betty Joseph (1989) is the best illustration of this point.

108 Ricoeur (1970), p.173.

109 '... the mother, the father, the boy's relations to them, the conflicts, the first love wounds – all these no longer exist except in the mode of a signified absence. If the artist's brush recreates the mother's smile in the smile of Mona Lisa, it must be said that the memory of it exists nowhere else but in this smile, itself unreal, of the Gioconda, which is signified only by the presence of the color and the pattern of the painting.' (Ricoeur, 1970, p.173). (see also Freud, 'Leonardo da Vinci and a Memory of his Childhood', *SE XI*.)

110 Freud, *Three Essays on Sexuality, SE VII*, and Laplanche and Pontalis (1980).

111 Ricoeur (1970), p.208.

112 Rustin (1991) makes the same point in his characterization of psychoanalysis as opposed to other 'talking cures' ('Psychoanalysis, Philosophical Realism and the New Sociology of Science').

113 I am relying here very much on the philosophical literature on Freud by Ricoeur (1965), Habermas (1978), Rieff (1960), Wollheim (1973), Draenos (1982) and Whitebook (1995), but there is a general agreement on this move even in the non-philosophical reading of Freud (Laplanche and Pontalis, 1980).

114 The term 'subconscious' was never used by Freud and it does not belong to psychoanalytical terminology. It was used by Pierre Janet in a different context from Freud's (see Brabant, 1971). The preconscious consisted of the ideas and affects not immediately present in consciousness, but readily available. There is no system of repression and censorship between preconsciousness and consciousness. The term perception-consciousness reinforces the role of this system as a sensory-perceptual receptor of information both from the outside and from the internal worlds (Laplanche and Pontalis, 1980, p.84).

115 Freud, *Introductory Lectures, SE XVI*, pp.295-6, also *Five Lectures on Psycho-Analysis, SE XI*, p.25.

116 'Thinking must concern itself with the connecting paths between ideas, without being led astray by the intensities of those ideas.' (Freud, *The Interpretation of Dreams, SE V*, p.602.)

117 'Actually the substitution of the reality principle for the pleasure principle implies no deposing of the pleasure principle, but only a safeguarding of it. A momentary pleasure, uncertain in its results, is given up, but only in order to gain along the new path an assured pleasure at a later time.' ('Formulations on the Two Principles of Mental Functioning' *SE XII*, p.223.)

118 'The individual does actually carry on a twofold existence: one to serve his own purposes and the other as a link in a chain ... He is the mortal vehicle of a (possibly) immortal substance ... The separation of the sexual instincts from the ego-instincts would simply reflect these two-fold

function of the individual.' ('On Narcissism: an Introduction', *SE XIV*); also Draenos (1982), Sulloway (1979).

119 'On Narcissism: an Introduction' *SE XIV*; Mitchell (1975), Wollheim (1985).
120 Two Encyclopedia Articles, *SE XVII*, p.415.
121 Laplanche and Pontalis (1980), p.147; Freud, *Three Essays on Sexuality*, *SE VII*.
122 Quoted by J. Mitchell (1975) p.31.
123 'On Narcissism: An Introduction.'
124 Ricoeur (1965), p.217; (1970), p.218, quotes Freud: 'Identification is known to psychoanalysis as the earliest expression of an emotional tie with another person' (*Group Psychology and the Analysis of the Ego*, *SE XVIII*, p.105).
125 Ricoeur (1965), p217; (1970), p.218; Freud, 'Identification' in *Group Psychology and the Analysis of the Ego*, *SE XVIII*.
126 Laplanche and Pontalis (1980), pp.141-2.
127 Whitebook (1992), p.108, *pace* Ricoeur (1965).
128 Freud, *New Introductory Lectures on Psycho-Analysis*, *SE XXII*, p.67.
129 Whitebook (1995).
130 See above, n.111, and Ricoeur (1970), p.208.
131 Freud, 'Analysis Terminable and Interminable', *SE XXIII*, p.243.
132 Marcuse (1966).
133 Segal (1978), Bléandonu (1985).
134 Klein, *The Psychoanalysis of Children* (1975, vol. II).
135 See Rustin (1991), p.147: 'The baby ... depended on the mother not only for its physical well-being, or even its sense of emotional comfort, but also for the development of its sense of identity and its powers of mental functioning.' Following Bion, contemporary Kleinians show how a certain type of thinking can be a non-thinking or even an attack on thinking, what Bion called 'minus k' or 'lies'.
136 Hinshelwood (1991), p.393.
137 Segal (1973), Hinshelwood (1991).
138 Segal (1973), p. 40.
139 See Hinshelwood (1991) on Kernberg, p.175.
140 Rustin (1991).
141 Benhabib (1992).
142 Benhabib (1992), p.156.
143 T. Hobbes, 'Philosophical Rudiments Concerning Government and Society', quoted by S. Benhabib, (1992), p.156.
144 Temperley (1997), p.265.
145 Segal (1973).
146 Alford (1989).
147 Segal (1978), Klein (1975).
148 Winch (1970).
149 Gadamer (1981).
150 Walzer (1983).
151 Habermas (1992), p.195.
152 Lyotard (1986).
153 'Among the essential features of this situation is that no one knows his place in society, his class position or his social status, nor does any one know his fortune in the distribution of natural assets and abilities, his intelligence, strength and the like. I shall even assume that the parties do not know their conceptions of the good or their special psychological propensities.' (Rawls, 1973, p.12).
154 'In searching for the most favored description of this situation we work from both ends. We begin by describing it so that it represents generally shared and preferably weak conditions. We then see if these conditions are strong enough to yield a significant set of principles. If not, we look for

further premises equally reasonable. But if so, and these principles match our considered convictions of justice, then so far well and good. But presumably there will be discrepancies. In this case, we have a choice. We can either modify the account of the initial situation or we can revise our existing judgements, for even the judgements we take provisionally as fixed points are liable to revision. By going back and forth, sometimes altering the conditions of the contractual circumstances, at others withdrawing our judgements and conforming them to principle, I assume that eventually we shall find a description of the initial situation that both expresses reasonable conditions and yields principles which match our considered judgement duly pruned and adjusted. This state of affairs I refer to as reflective equilibrium.' (Rawls, 1973, p.20.)

155 See Chapter 1.
156 Bernstein (1993).
157 'Life-forms, Morality and the Task of the Philosopher' in Dews (1986).
158 R. Rorty, 'Thugs and Theorists: A Reply to Bernstein' in *Political Theory, 15:1*, quoted by G. Warnke (1992).
159 Habermas (1992), p.23.
160 See above, Chapter 3.
161 Herrnstein and Murray (1994). For a different approach to intelligence, one that does not restrict it to purely formal-abstract features, and is indeed a critique of such restriction, see Gardner (1993).
162 Dworkin (1977).
163 Chapter 2 and Habermas (1984,1987a).
164 Habermas (1992), p.58.
165 Habermas (1973, 1992), McCarthy (1978).
166 'While there is an unequivocal relation between existing states of affairs and true propositions about them, the 'existence' or social currency of norms say nothing about whether the norms are valid. We must distinguish between the social fact that a norm is intersubjectively recognized and its worthiness to be recognized.' (Habermas, 1992, p. 61.).
167 Strawson (1974).
168 This is one of the reasons Habermas is so interested in Durkheim's work. Durkheim's understanding of sacrilege and other forms of primitive infringement of sanctions reveals the power of reasons in the social world. See Habermas, (1987a, 1992).
169 Habermas (1992), p.62.
170 Lyotard's attacks on Habermas are based on the latter's use of consensus as a guiding principle, a view that, Lyotard claims, overlooks the irreconcilable differences displayed in language.
171 In Habermas's words, 'every valid norm has to fulfil the following condition: (U) *All* affected can accept the consequences and the side effects its *general* observance can be anticipated to have for the satisfaction of *everyone's* interests (and these consequences are preferred to those of known alternative possibilities for regulation).' (Habermas, 1992, p. 65.)
172 See Chapter 2 above and Habermas (1979, 1984, 1987a).
173 Habermas (1992), McCarthy (1978).
174 Apel (1972, 1987).
175 Habermas (1992), Apel (1972, 1980, 1987).
176 Habermas (1992), p. 82.
177 The principle of discourse ethics (D) upholds that 'only those norms can claim to be valid that meet (or could meet) with the approval of all affected in their capacity as participants in a practical discourse.' (Habermas, 1992, p.93.)
178 As mentioned before, some Kleinians have argued, on the basis of ultra-sound research, that these relations start in fact in the womb of the mother. It is particularly interesting to read about twins, as they relate not only to their mother's body but also to each other, though one should be careful not to impose on these foetuses our fully formed ideals of a clear verbal conscience (Piontelli, 1992).
179 S. Freud, 'The Question of a Weltanschauung' in *New Introductory Lectures on Psychoanalysis, SE XVII.*
180 Warnke (1992).

181 Whitebook (1995), p.266.

182 Murphy and Gilligan (1980), Gilligan (1982).

183 Benhabib (1992).

184 See above, Chapter 2, and also Alvarez (1992), Bion (1977, 1988), O'Shaughnessy (1988, 1994).

185 see Britton *et al.* (1989).

186 For a review and critique of the feminist literature on this subject, see Benjamin (1998) and Temperley (1997). The latter gives a Kleinian reading of the same literature, which overcomes the dichotomies pointed by the former.

187 Klein 'The Oedipus complex in the light of early anxieties' (1945) in Britton *et al.* (1989).

188 'The Missing Link' in Britton *et al.* (1989).

189 Britton *et al.* (1989), p.87.

190 See Chapter 4, and Whitebook's reading of *Totem and Taboo* (1995) p.96.

191 For an overall account of Klein's theories and the problems raised by her critics, see Segal (1979) and Greenberg and Mitchell (1983).

192 Benhabib (1992).

193 'On the Genesis of Psychical Conflict in Early Infancy', in Rivière (1989), quoted by Alford (1989), p. 26.

194 Honneth (1995a).

195 See above, Chapter 1.

196 Lyotard (1986), Lyotard and Thébaud (1985), van Reijen and Veerman (1988), p.278): 'I can follow the line of Kantian thought, and also, to a very large extent, that of Wittgensteinian thought. Finding or trying to elaborate the rules which make the discourse of knowledge, for instance, possible – rules which we know to be under a general regime where truth or falsehood is at stake – is not the same as trying to elaborate the rules of a discourse, for example ethics, whose regime is one where good or evil, justice or injustice are at stake; nor is it the same thing for the discourse of aesthetics whose field of play is defined by the questions of beauty or ugliness ... .'

197 van Reijen and Veerman (1988), p.278.

198 Lyotard and Thébaud (1985).

199 Habermas (1978, 1980).

200 A similar point is made in Lyotard's critique of the Artificial Intelligence model, in *The Inhuman* (1991, pp.8-23), a critique which accepts H. Dreyfus's famous point that humans do not use solely binary logic, but a much richer situational framework where they are able to work imaginatively and intuitively. (Dreyfus, 1979.)

201 His critique of Marxism is the best example.

202 Lyotard and Thébaud (1985), Second Day.

203 Lyotard (1986).

204 'But ... whenever a story is told in this ethnic group, the teller always begins by saying: "I am going to tell you the story of X (here he inserts the name of the hero) as I have always heard it." And then he adds: "Listen to it!" In other words, he presents himself as having first been the addressee of a story of which he is now the teller. ... It is only at the end of the story ... that his name as a narrator, his proper name, is given. After, and not before. And what is striking is that when one of the listeners takes up the story some other time, he "forgets" the name of the previous narrator, since he does not give the name of the narrator who came before. One has "always heard it told."' (Lyotard and Thébaud (1985), p.32.

205 Lyotard and Thébaud (1985), p.32.

206 Lyotard and Thébaud (1985), p.34.

207 See above, Chapter 5.

208 Lyotard speaks of the 'risk of scepticism' of Derrida's position, which 'brings difference into play over all genres, all phrases, all linkages' (van Reijen and Veerman, 1988, p.287).

209 In the Preface of *The Differend*, Lyotard preaches the death of man and the death of the 'human sciences' as 'knowledge' built around the fiction of an autonomous subjectivity.

210 Especially in *The Differend* but see also his 'Presentations' in Montefiore (1983).

211 Lyotard (1991).

212 Levinas (1983, 1984), Hand (1992).

213 Levinas (1982, originally 1958).

214 Levinas, in Montefiore (1983), p.104.

215 'The relationship with the other is *time*: it is an untotalizable diachrony in which one moment pursues another without ever being able to retrieve it, to catch up with or coincide with it. The non-simultaneous and non-present is my primary rapport with the other in time. Time means that the other is forever beyond me, irreducible to the synchrony of the same. The temporality of the interhuman opens up the meaning of otherness and the otherness of meaning.' (E. Levinas, 'Ethics of the Infinite', in Kearney, 1984, p.57.)

216 Levinas, in Montefiore (1983), p.105.

217 Ibid, p.110. Also: 'Is this not the very meaning of the face, of the primordial speaking that *summons* me, questions me, stirs me, provokes my response or my responsibility, which – before any knowledge I may have of myself, before any reflexive presence of myself to myself, and beyond ny perseverance in Being and my repose in myself – would be the *for-the-other*, whereby the psychic life of humanity would be brought down to earth, and to a break with Heideggerian *Jemeinigkeit*?'

218 Simone de Beauvoir criticized Levinas' 'sexism' in *The Second Sex*, as she understood his assignation of the role of the 'other' to woman as a secondary, derivative status (see Levinas 1979, especially n.27, in Hand, 1992). The use we are making of the category of the 'other' points to another possible reading of this 'otherness', as a *challenge* to the narcissism, which generally presents the ideal subject as the autonomous Western white male, though the omnipotence and narcissism associated with the denial of our origins is not a male prerogative.

219 Vetlesen (1995).

220 '[Sartre] proclaims that 'the only point of departure possible is the Cartesian *cogito*', for 'the *cogito* alone establishes us on the ground of that factual necessity which is the necessity of the 'other's' existence' [*Being and Nothingness*, 338]. More specifically, whereas the *cogito* as we know it from Descartes's philosophy performs an affirmation of the indubitable truth of the fact that I exist, i.e., of my existence, the 'expanded' *cogito* Sartre has in mind here 'reveals to us as a fact the existence of the 'other' and my existence for the 'other' [*Being and Nothingness*, 376]' (A.J. Vetlesen, 1995, p.362).

221 See Chapter 5 and Britton (1995).

222 Hand (1992), Kearney (1984).

223 'The inhumanity of the system which is currently being consolidated under the name of development (among others) must not be confused with the infinitely secret one of which the soul is hostage. To believe, as it happened to me, that the first can take over from the second, give it expression, is a mistake.' (Lyotard, 1991, p.2.)

224 See above, n.31.

225 See above, n.26.

226 J. Habermas (1971), p. 120. For the full quotation, see n.62.

BIBLIOGRAPHY

Adorno, T. and Horkheimer, M. (1979) *Dialectic of Enlightenment*, London: Verso.

Alford, C.F. (1989) *Melanie Klein and Critical Social Theory*, Yale: Yale University Press.

Alvarez, A. (1992) *Live Company*, London: Routledge.

Apel, K.-O. (1972) 'The A Priori of Communication and the Foundation of Humanities' in *Man and World, 5*.

— (1980) 'The A Priori of the Communicative Community and the Foundations of Ethics' in K.-O. Apel, *Towards a Transformation of Philosophy*, London: Routledge and Kegan Paul.

— (1987) 'The Problem of Philosophical Foundations in Light of a Transcendental Pragmatics of Language' in K. Baynes *et al.* (eds), *After Philosophy*, Cambridge: M.I.T. Press.

Arendt, H. (1984) *Eichmann in Jerusalem: A Report on the Banality of Evil*, Harmondsworth: Penguin Books.

Austin, J.L. (1962) 'Performatif-Constatif' in *Cahiers de Royaumont: La philosophie analytique*, Paris.

— (1975) *How to Do Things with Words*, second edition, Oxford: Oxford University Press.

Baker, G.P. and Hacker, P.M.S. (1983a) *Wittgenstein Meaning and Understanding: Essays on the Philosophical Investigations*, Oxford: Blackwell.

— (1983b) *An Analytical Commentary on Wittgenstein's Philosophical Investigations*, Oxford: Blackwell.

— (1984) *Language, Sense and Nonsense*, Oxford: Blackwell.

Baudelaire, C. (1964) *The Painter of Modern Life and Other Essays*, translated and edited by J. Mayne, London: Phaidon.

Baynes, K.B. *et al.* (eds) (1987) *After Philosophy*, Cambridge, MA: M.I.T. Press.

Benhabib, S. (1992) 'The Generalized and the Concrete Other' in *Situating the Self*, Cambridge: Polity Press.

Benjamin, A. (ed) (1992), *Judging Lyotard*, London: Routledge

Benjamin, J. (1994) 'The Shadow of the Other (Subject): Intersubjectivity and Feminist Theory' in *Constellations, vol. 1, no. 2.*

— (1998) *Shadow of the Other: Intersubjectivity and Gender in Psychoanalysis*, New York and London: Routledge.

Bernstein, R. (1983) *Beyond Objectivism and Relativism*, Oxford: Blackwell.

— (ed) (1985) *Habermas and Modernity*, Cambridge: Polity Press.

— (1993) 'Splitting the Difference: In-Between Rorty and Habermas', unpublished paper presented at the Conference *La Modernité en question chez J. Habermas and R. Rorty*, Cerisy-la-Salle.

Bion, W.R. (1977) *Seven Servants*, New York: Jason Aronson.

— (1988) 'Attacks on Linking' in E.B. Spillius, *Melanie Klein Today, vol. 1: Mainly Theory*, London: Routledge.

Bléandonu, G. (1985) *L'école de Melanie Klein*, Paris: Le Centurion.

Brabant, G.P. (1971) *Clefs pour la psychanalyse*, Paris: Seghers.

Britton, R. *et al.* (1989) *The Oedipus Complex Today*, London: Karnac Books.

Buck-Morss, S. (1982) 'Socio-Economic Bias in Piaget's Theory and its Implications for Cross-Cultural Studies' in S. and C. Modgil (eds), *Jean Piaget: Consensus and Controversy*, New Jersey: Holt, Rinehart and Winston.

Castoriadis, C. (1975) *L'institution imaginaire de la société*, Paris: Seuil.

— (1978) *Les Carrefours du Labyrinthe*, Paris: Seuil.

Chomsky, N. (1970) *Aspects of the Theory of Syntax*, Cambridge, MA: M.I.T. Press.

Cohen, J. (1989) 'Heller, Habermas and Justice' in *Praxis International, vol. VIII, no.4.*

Cole, P. and Morgan, J. (eds) (1975) *Syntax and Semantics (vol. III): Speech Acts*, London: Academic Press.

Dallmayr, F. (1972) 'Reason and Emancipation: Notes on Habermas' in *Man and World, 5.*

Dallmayr, F. and McCarthy, T. (eds) (1977) *Understanding and Social Inquiry*, Notre Dame: University of Notre Dame Press.

Derrida, J. (1977) 'Signature, Event, Context' in I. Glyph *Baltimore: The Johns Hopkins Press.*

— (1986) *Memoires for Paul de Man*, New York: Columbia University Press.

Derrida, J. *et al.* (1985) *La faculté de juger*, Paris: Minuit.

Descartes, R. (1970) *Méditations*, in *Oeuvres et lettres*, Paris: Bibliothèque de la Pléiade.

— (1998) *Meditations and Other Metaphysical Writings*, London: Penguin Books.

Dews, P. (ed) (1986) *Habermas, Autonomy and Solidarity – Interviews*, London: Verso.

Draenos, S. (1982) *Freud's Odyssey*, New Haven and London: Yale University Press.

Dreyfus, H. (1979) *What Computers Can't Do*, New York: Harper Colophon Books.

Dworkin, R. (1977) 'Justice and Rights' in *Taking Rights Seriously*, Cambridge: Harvard University Press.

Edwards, J. (1982) *Ethics without Philosophy: Wittgenstein and the Moral Life*, Tampa: University Press of Florida.

Fahrenbach, H. (ed) (1973) *Wirklichkeit und Reflexion*, Pfullingen: Neske.

Felman, S. (1983) *The Literary Speech Act: Don Juan with J. L. Austin or Seduction in Two Languages*, Ithaca: Cornell University Press.

Figueira, S. (1984) *The Study of Psychoanalytical Diffusion*, Ph.D. dissertation: University of London.

Figueira, S. (ed) (1988) *Efeito Psi – A Influência da Psicanálise*, Rio de Janeiro: Campos.

Foucault, M. (1974) *A Verdade e as Formas Juridicas, Cadernos da PUC/RJ no. 16*, Rio de Janeiro: Pontificia Universidade Catolica.

Freeman, D. (1983) *Margaret Mead in Samoa: The Making and Unmaking of an Anthropological Myth*, Cambridge, MA: Harvard University Press.

Freud, S. (1975) 'The Interpretation of Dreams', in *Standard Edition, vol. V*; 'Three Essays on Sexuality', in *vol. VII*; 'Five Lectures on Psychoanalysis, Leonardo da Vinci and Other Works', in vol. XI; 'Formulations on the Two Principles of Mental Functioning', in *vol. XII*; 'Recommendations to Physicians Practising Analysis', in vol. XII; 'Remembering, Repeating and Working Through', in *vol. XII*; 'Totem and Taboo', in vol. XIII,

'Instincts and their Vicissitudes', in *vol. XIV*; 'On Narcissism: an Introduction', *vol. XIV*; 'The Unconscious', in *On Metapsychology*, *vol. XIV*; 'Introductory Lectures on Psychoanalysis', in *vol. XVI*; 'Beyond the Pleasure Principle', in *vol. XVII*; 'A Difficulty in the Path of Psychoanalysis', in *vol. XVII*; 'Two Encyclopedia Articles', in vol. XVII; 'Group Psychology and the Analysis of the Ego', in *vol. XVIII*; 'The Ego and the Id', in *vol. XIX*; 'An Autobiographical Study', in *vol. XX*; 'The Future of an Illusion', in *vol. XXI*; 'New Introductory Lectures on Psychoanalysis', in *vol. XXII*; 'Analysis Terminable and Interminable', in *vol. XXIII*, , London: The Hogarth Press and the Institute of Psychoanalysis.

Frisby, D. (1985) *Fragments of Modernity*, Cambridge: Polity Press.

Gadamer, H.-G. (1981) *Truth and Method*, London: Sheed and Ward.

— (1987) *Philosophical Hermeneutics*, Berkeley: University of California Press.

Gardner, H. (1993) *Frames of Mind – The Theory of Multiple Intelligences*, New York: Basic Books.

Gilligan, C. (1982) *In a Different Voice: Psychological Theory and Women's Development*, Cambridge, MA: Harvard University Press.

Greenberg, J. and Mitchell, S. (1983) *Object Relations in Psychoanalytical Theory*, Cambridge, MA: Harvard University Press.

Grosskurth, P. (1986) *Melanie Klein – Her World and Her Work*, London: Hodder & Stoughton.

Habermas, J. (1970a) 'On Systematically Distorted Communication' in *Inquiry*, 13.

— (1970b) 'Towards a Theory of Communicative Competence' in *Inquiry*, 13.

— (1971) 'Vorbereitende Bemerkungen zu einer Theorie der kommunikativen Kompetenz' in J. Habermas and N. Luhman, *Theorie der Gesellschaft oder Sozialtechnologie*, Frankfurt: Suhrkamp.

— (1973) 'Wahrheitstheorien' in H. Fahrenbach (ed), *Wirklichkeit und Reflexion*, Pfullingen: Neske.

— (1975) 'Sprachspiel, Intention und Bedeutung: zu Motiven bei Sellars and Wittgenstein' in R. Wiggerhaus (ed) *Sprachanalyse und Soziologie: die Sozialwissenschaftliche Relevanz von Wittgensteins Sprachphilosophie*, Frankfurt: Suhrkamp.

— (1977) 'A Review of Gadamer's *Truth and Method* in F. Dallmayr and T. McCarthy (eds), *Understanding and Social Inquiry*, Notre Dame: University of Notre Dame Press.

— (1978) *Knowledge and Human Interests, second edition*, London, Heinemann.

— (1979) 'What is Universal Pragmatics?' in J. Habermas, *Communication and the Evolution of Society*, London: Heinemann.

— (1980) 'Technology and Science as "Ideology"' in J. Habermas, *Toward a Rational Society*, London: Heinemann.

— (1981) 'Modernity versus Postmodernity' in *New German Critique, 22*.

— (1983) *Philosophical-Political Profiles*, Cambridge, MA: M.I.T. Press.

— (1984) *The Theory of Communicative Action, vol. I*, Boston: Beacon Press.

— (1987a) *The Theory of Communicative Action, vol. II*, Boston: Beacon Press.

— (1987b) *The Philosophical Discourse of Modernity*, Cambridge: Polity Press.

— (1992) *Moral Consciousness and Communicative Action*, Oxford: Blackwell.

Habermas, J. and Luhman, N. (1971) *Theorie der Gesellschaft oder Sozialtechnologie*, Frankfurt: Suhrkamp.

Hamilton, V. (1982) *Narcissus and Oedipus – The Children of Psychoanalysis*, London: Karnac Books.

Hand, S. (1992) (ed) *The Levinas Reader*, London: Blackwell.

Havel, V. (1985) 'The Power of the Powerless' in J. Keane (ed), *The Power of the Powerless*, New York: M.E. Sharpe, Inc.

Heimann, P. (1989) 'On Countertransference' in M. Tonnesman (ed), *Children and Children No Longer – Collected Papers of Paula Heimann*, London: Routledge.

Herrnstein, R. and Murray, C. (1994) *The Bell Curve*, New York: Simon & Schuster.

Hinshelwood, R. (1991) *A Dictionary of Kleinian Thought*, London: Free Association Books.

Honneth, A. (1995a) 'The Other of Justice' in S. White (ed), *Cambridge Companion to Habermas*, Cambridge: Cambridge University Press.

— (1995b) 'Decentered Autonomy: The Subject after the Fall' in *The Fragmented World of the Social*, Suny Press.

Husserl, E. (1977) *Cartesian Meditations*, The Hague: Martinus Nijhoff.

Hymes, D. (1980) 'On Communicative Competence' in A.F. Pugh *et al.* (eds), *Language and Language Use*, London: Heinemann.

Isaacs, S. (1989) 'The Nature and Function of Phantasy' in J. Rivière (ed), *Developments in Psychoanalysis*, London: Karnac Books.

Jauss, H. R. (1970) *Literaturgeschichte als Provokation*, Frankfurt: Surkhamp.

Joseph, B. (1989) *Psychic Equilibrium and Psychic Change*, London: Tavistock/Routledge.

Kant, I. (1951) *Critique of Judgement*, New York: Hafner Press.

— (1970) 'An Answer to the Question : "What is Enlightenment?"' in H. Reiss (ed),s *Kant's Political Writings*, Cambridge: Cambridge University Press.

— (1982) *Critique of Practical Reason*, Indianapolis: Bobbs-Merrill.

— (1996) *Critique of Pure Reason*, Indianapolis/Cambridge: Hackett Publishing Co.

Keane, J. (ed) (1985) *The Power of the Powerless*, New York: M.E. Sharpe, Inc.

Kearney, R. (1984) *Dialogues with Contemporary Continental Thinkers*, Manchester: Manchester University Press.

King, P. (1989) 'Preface' in M. Tonnesman (ed), *Children and Children No Longer – Collected Papers of Paula Heimann*, London: Routledge.

Klein, M. (1975) *The Writings of Melanie Klein, 4 vols. Vol. I: Love, Guilt and Reparation and Other Works, 1921-1945; Vol. II: The Psychoanalysis of Children; Vol. III : Envy and Gratitude and Other Works 1946-1963; Vol. IV: Narrative of a Child Analysis.*

Kuhn, T. (1970) *The Structure of Scientific Revolutions,* 2nd edition, Chicago: University of Chicago Press.

Kuper, A. (1989) 'Coming of Age in Anthropology' in *Nature, vol. 338.*

Laplanche, J. and Pontalis, J.-B. (1980) *The Language of Psychoanalysis*, London: The Hogarth Press.

Levinas, E. (1958) 'Martin Buber and the Theory of Knowledge' in S. Hand (ed), *The Levinas Reader*, London: Blackwell.

— (1979) 'Time and the Other' in S. Hand (ed), *The Levinas Reader*, London: Blackwell.

— (1983) 'Beyond Intentionality' in A. Montefiore, (ed) *Philosophy in France Today*, Cambridge: Cambridge University Press.

— (1984) 'Ethics of the Infinite' in R. Kearney, *Dialogues with Contemporary Continental Thinkers*, Manchester: Manchester University Press.

Lyotard, J.-F. (1954) *La Phénoménologie*, Paris: P.U.F.

— (1971) *Discours, Figure*, Paris: Klincksieck.

— (1974) *Economie libidinale*, Paris: Minuit.

— (1983) *Des dispositifs pulsionnels*, second edition, Paris: Christian Bourgeois.

— (1986) *The Postmodern Condition*, Manchester: Manchester University Press.

— (1986b) *Le postmoderne expliqué aux enfants*, Paris: Galilée.

114

— (1988) *The Differend – Phrases in Dispute*, Minnesota: University of Minnesota Press.

— (1991) *The Inhuman*, Cambridge: Polity Press.

— (1993) *Political Writings*, Minnesota: University of Minnesota Press.

Lyotard, J.-F and Thébaud J.L. (1985) *Just Gaming (Au Juste)*, Minnesota: Minnesota University Press.

McCarthy, T. (1978) *The Critical Theory of Jürgen Habermas*, Cambridge, MA: M.I.T. Press.

Maclean, I. *et al.* (eds) (1990) *The Political Responsibility of Intellectuals*, Cambridge: Cambridge University Press.

Masson, J. (1985) *The Assault on Truth*, Harmondsworth: Penguin Books.

Marcuse, H. (1996) *Eros and Civilization: A Philosophical Inquiry into Freud*, Boston: Beacon Press.

— (1977) *Reason and Revolution*, London: Routledge and Kegan Paul.

— (1986) *One-Dimensional Man*, London: Routledge and Kegan Paul.

Meisel P. and Kendrick, W. (1986) *Bloomsbury/Freud: The Letters of James and Alix Strachey 1924-1925*, London: Chatto & Windus.

Mendelson, P. (1979) 'The Habermas–Gadamer Debate' in *New German Critique, 18*.

Modgil S. and C. (eds) (1982) *Jean Piaget: Consensus and Controversy*, New Jersey: Holt, Rinehart and Winston.

Montefiore, A. (ed) (1983) *Philosophy in France Today*, Cambridge: Cambridge University Press.

— (1990) 'The Political Responsibility of Intellectuals' in I. Maclean *et al.* (eds), *The Political Responsibility of Intellectuals*, Cambridge: Cambridge University Press.

Merleau-Ponty, M. (1980) *Humanisme et Terreur*, Paris: Gallimard.

— (1985) *Phénoménologie de la perception*, Paris: Gallimard.

Mitchell, J. (1974) *Psychoanalysis and Feminism*, Harmondsworth: Penguin.

Murphy J. M. and Gilligan, C. (1980) 'Moral Development in Late Adolescence and Adulthood: A Critique and Reconstruction of Kohlberg's Theory', in *Human Development, 23*.

Nancy, J.-L. (1985) 'Dies Irae' in J. Derrida *et al.*, *La faculté de juger*, Paris: Minuit.

O'Shaughnessy, E. (1988) 'W.R. Bion's Theory of Thinking and New Techniques in Child Analysis' in E. Spillius (ed), *Melanie Klein Today, Vol. II – Mainly Practice*, London: Routledge.

— (1994) 'What is a Clinical Fact?' in D. Tuckett (ed) *The Conceptualization and Communication of Clinical facts in Psychoanalysis, International Journal of Psychoanalysis, vol. 75,*

Piatelli-Palmarini, M. (ed), (1979) *Théories du langage – Théories de l'apprentissage (Le débat entre Jean Piaget et Noam Chomsky)*, Paris: Seuil.

Piontelli, A. (1992) *From Foetus to Child: An Observational and Psychoanalytical Study*, London: Routledge.

Pugh, A.F. *et al.* (eds) (1980) *Language and Language Use*, London: Heinemann.

Raphael-Leff, J. and Perelberg, R. (1997) (eds), *Female Experience – Three Generations of British Women Psychoanalysts on Work with Women*, London: Routledge.

Rawls, J. (1973) *A Theory of Justice*, Oxford: Oxford University Press.

Ricoeur, P. (1965) *De l'Interprétation – un essai sur Freud*, Paris: Seuil.

— (1970) *Freud and Philosophy: an Essay on Interpretation*, New Haven and London: Yale University Press.

— (1973) 'Ethics and Culture – Habermas and Gadamer in Dialogue' in *Philosophy Today, 17*.

Rivière, J. (ed) (1989), *Developments in Psychoanalysis*, London: Karnac Books.

Rieff, P. (1960) *Freud – The Mind of a Moralist*, London: Victor Gollancz.

Rorty, R. (1980) *Philosophy and the Mirror of Nature*, Oxford: Blackwell.

— (1985) 'Habermas and Lyotard on Postmodernity' in R. Bernstein (ed.) *Habermas and Modernity*, Cambridge: Polity Press.

G. Runcimon (ed) (1978) *Max Weber: Selections in Translation*, Cambridge, Cambridge University Press.

Rustin, M, (1991) *The Good Society and the Inner World*, London: Verso.

Sartre, J.-P. (1968) *Being and Nothingness*, New York: Citadel Press.

— (1985) *The Freud Scenario* J. B. Pontalis (ed), London: Verso.

Searle, J. (1972) *Speech Acts*, Cambridge: Cambridge University Press.

— (1979) *Expression and Meaning*, Cambridge: Cambridge University Press.

Segal, H. (1978) *Introduction to the Work of Melanie Klein*.

— (1981) 'Notes on Symbol Formation' in *The Work of Hanna Segal*, London: Jason Aronson.

Spillius, E. B. (ed.) (1988a) *Melanie Klein Today, Vol. I – Mainly Theory*, London: Routledge.

— (1988b) *Melanie Klein Today, Vol. II – Mainly Practice*, London: Routledge.

Stampe, D. (1975) 'Meaning and Truth in the Theory of Speech Acts' in P. Cole and J. Morgan (eds), *Syntax and Semantics, vol. 3 Speech Acts*, London: Academic Press.

Steiner, J. (1993) 'Two Types of Pathological Organization in *Oedipus the King* and *Oedipus at Colonus*' in *Psychic Retreats*, London: Routledge.

Stern, D. (1985) *The Interpersonal World of the Infant*, New York: Basic Books.

Steuerman, E. (1985) *Habermas's 'Universal Pragmatics': an Overview*, Ph.D. dissertation: University of London.

— (1988) 'Habermas e a Psicanálise' in S. Figueirs (ed), *Efeito Psi – A Influência da Psicanálise*, Rio de Janeiro: Campos.

— (1992) 'Habermas vs Lyotard: Modernity vs Postmodernity?' in A. Benjamin (ed), *Judging Lyotard*, London: Routledge.

Strawson, P. (1974) *Freedom and Resentment*, London: Methuen.

Sulloway, F. (1979) *Freud Biologist of the Mind*, London: Burnett Books.

Temperley, J. (1997) 'Is the Oedipus Complex Bad News for Women?' in J. Raphael-Leff and R. Perelberg (eds), *Female Experience – Three Generations of British Women Psychoanalysts on Work with Women*, London: Routledge.

Thompson, J. B. (1982). 'Universal Pragmatics' in J. B. Thompson and D. Held (eds), *Critical Debates*, London: The Macmillan Press.

Thompson, J. B. and Held, D. (eds) (1982), *Critical Debates*, London: The Macmillan Press.

Tonnesmann, M. (ed.) (1989) *Children and Children-No-Longer: Collected Papers of Paula Heimann*, London: Routledge.

Trevarthen, C. (1986) 'Development of Intersubjective Motor Control in Infants' in G.M. Wade and H.G.A. White (eds), *Motor Development in Children: Aspects of Coordination and Control*, Dordrecht: Martinus Nijhof.

Tuckett, D. (ed) (1994) *The Conceptualization and Communication of Clinical Facts in Psychoanalysis, International Journal of Psychoanalysis, vol. 75*.

van Reijen and Veerman (1988) 'An Interview with Jean-François Lyotard' in *Society, 5*.

Vetlesen, A. J. (1995) 'Relations with Others in Sartre and Levinas' in *Constellations, vol.1, no. 3*.

Vygotsky, L. S. (1979) *Thought and Language*, Cambridge, MA: M.I.T. Press.

Walzer, M. (1983) *Spheres of Justice*, New York: Basic Books.

Warnke, G. (1992) *Justice and Interpretation*, Cambridge, Polity Press.

Weber, M. (1978) 'Protestant Asceticism and the Spirit of Capitalism' in G. Runcimon (ed.) *Max Weber: Selections in Translation*, Cambridge: Cambridge University Press.

Wellmer, A. (1981) *The Persistence of Modernity*, Cambridge: Polity Press.

Wilson, B. (1970) *Rationality*, Oxford: Blackwell.

Winch, P. (1970) 'Understanding a Primitive Society' in B. Wilson, *Rationality*, Oxford: Blackwell.

White, S. (ed) (1995) *Cambridge Companion to Habermas*, Cambridge: Cambridge University Press.

Whitebook, J. (1992) 'Reflections on the Autonomous Individual and the Decentered Subject' in *American Imago*, vol. 49, no 1.

— (1995) *Perversion and Utopia*, Cambridge, MA: M.I.T. Press.

Wiggerhaus, R. (ed.) (1975) *Sprachanalyse und Soziologie: die Sozialwissenschaftliche Relevanz von Wittgensteins Sprachphilosophie*, Frankfurt: Suhrkamp.

Winnicott, D. (1976) *The Maturational Processes and the Facilitating Environment: Studies in the Theory of Emotional Development*, London: The Hogarth Press.

Wittgenstein, L. (1974) *Philosophical Investigations*, Oxford: Blackwell.

Wolheim, R. (1973) *Freud*, London: Fontana Press.

INDEX

Adorno, Theodor 6; and art 2, 109n 6; and the conscious and unconscious 47
Alford, C.F. 86
Anciens, disputes with *Modernes* and modernist consciousness 2–3, 109n 8
Apel, K.-O., and performative contradiction 80
Arendt, Hannah, and Eichmann's inability to relate 35
argumentative reasoning 32
art 2
Au Juste (Just Gaming) (Lyotard and Thébaud) 87–8, 89
Aulus Gellius 112–13n 77
Austin, J.L., speech act theory 27–8
autism, and relating 34
Azanda people 72–3

Baudelaire, Charles Pierre 113n 89; and modernity 3, 4, 109n 9; and time 48, 49
Bell Curve (Herrnstein and Murray) 76
Benhabib, Seyla: ethics of care 86; narcissism and social theory 68–9; and universalism 83
Beyond the Pleasure Principle (Freud) 55
Bion, W.R. 19, 45; and relating 33, 34
body, Lyotard's concern with rationalism 10, 13–14, 110n 27
Boileau, Nicolas 3
Borges, J.L. xi
Brazil, philosophy students' understanding of truth and science xi
Brentano, Franz Clemens 33

care, ethics 86
caritas (love), Klein's understanding 70, 71, 99
Cartesianism: knowledge theories 1–2; *see*
also Descartes, René
Cashinahua Indians, narratives 48, 89–91
Categorical Imperative 74
children: and the inhuman 96–7; and psychoanalysis 63–6
Chomsky, N., competence theory and language 23–5
communication: and language 11–12, 14, 20–1, 27–32, 49–50; and psychoanalysis 31–6; *see also* discourse; language
communicative competence, Habermas's view 77–8
competence theory and language, Chomsky's views 23–5
conscious: formation 2–3; and phenomenology 7–9; and the unconscious 41, 42–3, 46–7; *see also* unconscious
conscious-preconscious, and the unconscious 55–6, 114n 117
consensus, Habermas's understanding 22–6, 29–30
constatives 27
countertransference 16–17, 19, 20
cultural situation, and justice 75–6, 115–16n 155
culture, and instincts 62
cultures, values and understanding these values 72–4

da Vinci, Leonardo, *La Gioconda* 54
Dallmayr, F. 13, 26
d'Ans, André Marcel, *Dits des Vrais Hommes* 89
de Beauvoir, Simone, criticizes Levinas's sexism 118n 219
de Man, Paul 8

time: and knowledge 39–40; and
  modernity 4, 48–9, 109n 12; and
  narrative 89–90; and otherness 93,
  118n 216
totalitarianism 47
Totem and Taboo (Freud) 60
'Towards a Theory of Communicative
  Competence' (Habermas) 23, 24
tradition, Lyotard's views 89
transference 16, 19, 20
truth: and communication through
  language 28–31; Foucault's views xi;
  and language xi–xiii; Lyotard's
  approach to 87–8; as perverted by
  narratives 47–8; and science xi–xii
Truth and Method (Gadamer) 8
types theory 39

unconscious 10–11, 12, 13–20; and the
  conscious 41, 42–3, 46–7, 59–60;
  Freud's views xvi, 51, 52; and
  psychoanalysis 51; *see also* conscious
understanding: and historicality 8; and
  psychoanalysis 46–7

'Understanding a Primitive Culture'
  (Winch) 72
universalism: as affected by language
  75–80; Benhabib's views 83
universalization principle 79–86; and the
  other 98
'Universal Pragmatics' (Habermas) 30, 32
unknown, Freud's use 97

veil of ignorance, Rawls's theory 74–5, 77
Vetlesen, J., and otherness 94

Warnke, G. 82–3
Weber, Max 2
Whitebook, J. 60, 83
Winch, Peter, culture and moral judgement
  72
Winnicott, D., and relating 33
wishful impulses 41
Wittgenstein, Ludwig 39; language games
  23, 24, 25; and understanding of the
  unconscious 46
working-through 97
'Working Through' (Freud) 46